Growing Up in Canada

Other titles in the *Growing Up Around the World* series include:

Growing Up in Brazil
Growing Up in China
Growing Up in Germany
Growing Up in India
Growing Up in Iran
Growing Up in Italy
Growing Up in Japan
Growing Up in Mexico
Growing Up in Russia

Growing Up in Canada

Gail Snyder

San Diego, CA

© 2018 ReferencePoint Press, Inc.
Printed in the United States

For more information, contact:
ReferencePoint Press, Inc.
PO Box 27779
San Diego, CA 92198
www.ReferencePointPress.com

ALL RIGHTS RESERVED.
No part of this work covered by the copyright hereon may be reproduced or used in any form or by any means—graphic, electronic, or mechanical, including photocopying, recording, taping, web distribution, or information storage retrieval systems—without the written permission of the publisher.

LIBRARY OF CONGRESS CATALOGING-IN-PUBLICATION DATA

Name: Snyder, Gail, author.
Title: Growing Up in Canada/by Gail Snyder.
Description: San Diego, CA: ReferencePoint Press, Inc., 2018. | Series: Growing Up Around the World series | Includes bibliographical references and index.
Identifiers: LCCN 2017022755 (print) | LCCN 2017024030 (ebook) | ISBN 9781682822081 (eBook) | ISBN 9781682822074 (hardback)
Subjects: LCSH: Canada—Social life and customs—Juvenile literature. | Youth—Canada—Juvenile literature. | Families—Canada—Juvenile literature.
Classification: LCC F1021.2 (ebook) | LCC F1021.2 .S625 2018 (print) | DDC 971—dc23
LC record available at https://lccn.loc.gov/2017022755

CONTENTS

Canada at a Glance	6
Chapter One Where Differences Are Celebrated	8
Chapter Two Families in Transition	20
Chapter Three Education and Work	31
Chapter Four Social Life	43
Chapter Five Hopes and Challenges	55
Source Notes	68
For Further Research	73
Index	75
Picture Credits	79
About the Author	80

CANADA AT A GLANCE

Official Name
Canada

Capital
Ottawa

Size
3,855,101 square miles
(9,984,666 sq. km)

Total Population
35,362,905 as of 2016

Youth Population
0–14 years: 15.44%
15–24 years: 12.12%

Religion
Catholic: 39%; Protestant: 20.3%; Muslim: 3.2%; Hindu: 1.5%; Sikh: 1.4%; Buddhist: 1.1%; Jewish: 1%; other: 0.6%

Type of Government
Parliamentary democracy and constitutional monarchy

Language
English (58.7%), French (22%), plus at least eight other languages

Currency
Canadian dollar

Industries
Automobiles, agriculture, technology, energy, chemicals, food processing

Literacy
97%

Internet Users
31,053,000, or 88.5% of population

CHAPTER ONE

Where Differences Are Celebrated

When many people think of Canada, they may picture people who are polite and friendly but who, nevertheless, pronounce the word *about* as though it is spelled *aboot*. They may also find themselves thinking about the ranks of professional ice hockey, which are dominated by Canadian players. Or the familiar Canadian toque (sometimes spelled *tuque* or *touque*), a knit cap that is vital to surviving the cold Canadian winters. Another familiar symbol of Canada is the Royal Canadian Mounted Police—officers wearing red tunics and patrolling, on horseback, the vast wilderness of the Yukon. But there is a lot more to Canada than these familiar images.

Canada is a celebration of many cultures: a global stew in which French, British, Scottish, Asian Indian, Chinese, and other peoples have come together but still retain their individual identities. For young people, this multiculturalism has an impact on their lives through the way their government works, the symphony of languages they hear spoken, the differing traditions they see embraced, and the way immigrants are made welcome without being pressured to become "Canadian."

Perhaps Canadian prime minister Justin Trudeau summed it up best when he said that being Canadian is more about shared values than it is about having a single national character. "There is no core identity, no mainstream in Canada," said Trudeau. "There are shared values—openness, respect, compassion, willingness to work hard, to be there for each other, to search for equality and justice."[1]

Big Differences in Geography

Among the Canadian people, these traits can be found throughout the country's huge landmass. Encompassing 3.8 million square miles (9.9 million sq. km), Canada is second only to Russia in total landmass. Canada is America's next-door neighbor. The border between the continental United States and Canada spans some 5,500 miles (8,851 km).

The Canadian border abuts the states of Washington, Idaho, Montana, North Dakota, Minnesota, Wisconsin, Michigan, New York, Vermont, New Hampshire, and Maine. (Technically, Ohio and Pennsylvania also share a border with Canada; these states are separated from the Canadian mainland by Lake Erie, ownership of which is shared by the two countries.) Moreover, Canada shares its western border with Alaska. The Alaska-Canada border runs some 1,500 miles (2,416 km).

Canada is a nation of ten provinces, which are similar to US states. They include Alberta, British Columbia, Manitoba, New Brunswick, Newfoundland and Labrador, Nova Scotia, Ontario, Prince Edward Island, Quebec, and Saskatchewan. In addition, Canada is home to three territories—vast, sparsely populated regions that have no provincial governments of their own and are administered by the federal Canadian government. These regions are the Yukon, Nunavut, and the Northwest Territories. Of the more than 35 million people who live in Canada, only about 100,000 make their homes in the three territories—and it is easy to see why. Portions of all three territories lie north of the Arctic Circle.

Surrounded by Water

Except for its border with the United States, the country is surrounded by water: the Atlantic Ocean, Labrador Sea, and Baffin Bay to the east; the Pacific Ocean and Gulf of Alaska to the west; and the Beaufort Sea and Arctic Ocean to the north. In addition, Canada has more than half the world's lakes. Such prodigious water sources are useful for providing drinking water and hydroelectric power. Tourists flock to Canada, attracted by the country's beautiful waterways and seaside landscapes. Indeed, Canada shares Niagara Falls with the state of New York; yet it is Horseshoe Falls, located on the Canadian side, that is regarded as the most majestic and picturesque part of Niagara Falls.

In addition to water, Canada is home to many mountain chains—the Rocky, Coast, Laurentian, and Appalachian Mountains—as well as plains, islands, prairies, swampy lowlands, forests, and glaciers.

Horseshoe Falls (pictured) is just one of many beautiful waterways and scenic landscapes found in Canada. The country's extraordinarily diverse landscape includes mountains, plains, forests, swamps, glaciers, and islands.

Canada is home to 80 percent of the world's polar bears. Other wildlife roaming the Canadian wilderness are bison, beavers, moose, and reindeer. Blue whales can be found along the coastlines.

Along with these natural features, Canada has deposits of natural gas, petroleum, gold, silver, and copper that can be mined and exported. The country's vast forestland enables Canadian companies to export lumber and paper. In fact, Canada has substantially more forest acreage (34.1 percent) than it does land devoted to raising food products (5.8 percent). Farmers grow wheat, rye, soybeans, barley, and other grains. Ranchers raise cattle, and commercial fishing vessels harvest fish in natural bodies of water and through offshore fish farms.

Variations in climate also impact where people live. For example, northern Canada has experienced temperatures as low as -81°F (-62°C). Temperatures moderate farther south. In fact, most of Canada's residents live in the southern portion of the country, within about 100 miles (161 km) of the US border.

In terms of population, the two largest provinces are Ontario and Quebec, with more than 21 million of the country's 35 million citizens. Most residents of the two provinces live in or near the country's two largest cities, Toronto (in Ontario) and Montreal (in Quebec). Two-thirds of the country's 2.8 million teenagers live in the two cities or their suburbs. Teenagers who live in those cities and others—among them Calgary and Edmonton in Alberta, Winnipeg in Manitoba, and Vancouver in British Columbia—have no shortage of activities to fill their time. They ride bikes, visit museums, play laser tag, ice skate, play ice hockey, or go to the movies.

The Birth of Kanata

As with teenagers most everywhere, a lot of their time is taken up with schoolwork. And early in their educations, young Canadians learn about the history of their nation. It is a history that dates back to the 1600s, when French and British explorers arrived in the New World. (The first settlement in Canada was established in 1604 by French explorer Pierre de Monts in Nova Scotia.) When the French and British arrived, they relied on native people to show them the land. These native peoples who hunted, fished, and farmed had their own languages and cultures but were totally unprepared for the onslaught of foreign invaders. Initially interested in finding a passage to Asia, the explorers were soon attracted to Canada's natural resources, including its abundant fish, furs, and trees. Their guides—indigenous people now referred to as First Nation people—used the word *Kanata*, which means "village, or settlement." The Europeans soon referred to the land they were exploring as Kanata (and, eventually, Canada).

To some degree, the history of Canada is tied directly to the history of the United States. When the French and Indian War erupted in 1754—a conflict between the French and British for control of the North American continent—Canada was the scene of many battles. Most notable is the Battle of Sainte-Foy in Quebec in 1760, in which the British army was routed by the French in what would be the final French victory in the war. Nevertheless, in 1763 Great Britain claimed victory in the war, and among the prizes seized by the British was control of Canada.

Still, Quebec and the city of Montreal have retained their French identity because the French citizens living there opted to remain after the British gained control of Canada. Quebecers—in French, the Quebecois—have maintained their language, culture, and religion. Under British rule, immigrants from England, Scotland, Wales, and Ireland soon arrived. Canada achieved self-rule in 1867—not through an armed revolution but rather through diplomacy and negotiations. "We didn't do it by going to war. We

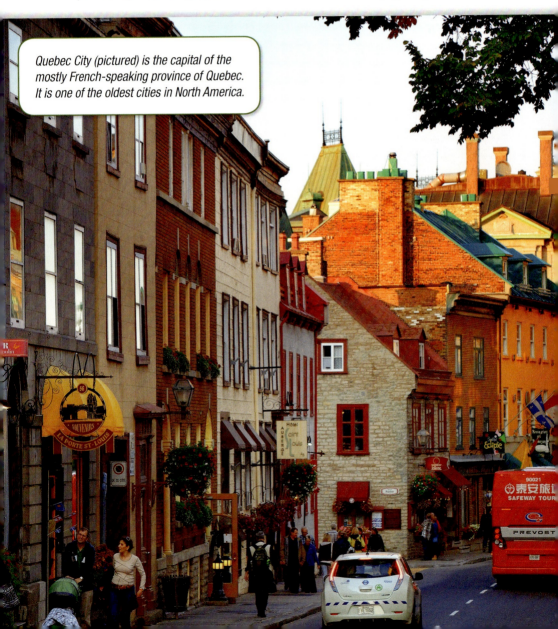

Quebec City (pictured) is the capital of the mostly French-speaking province of Quebec. It is one of the oldest cities in North America.

went to England and convinced them that they should let us be a country, and so we worked with them,"² says Stuart McNish, host of the Canadian public television program *Conversations That Matter*.

The Canadian Government

What resulted from those events is a twofold system of government: a parliamentary democracy and a constitutional monarchy. Although Queen Elizabeth II is Canada's head of state, the prime minister heads the government. The prime minister presides over Parliament, the body that is entrusted with running the federal government. Parliament consists of the queen, the Senate, and the House of Commons. Members of the Senate are appointed by the governor-general, acting as representative of the queen. Members of the House of Commons are elected by voters. Whichever political party wins the majority of seats in the House of Commons chooses the prime minister. The prime minister and Parliament perform their duties in Ottawa, the nation's capital, located in Ontario.

Parliament presides over national and international affairs. For instance, it is responsible for maintaining the military, securing trade agreements with other countries, and maintaining roads, rivers, and other transportation systems. It is also responsible for banking, taxes, and mail.

> "We didn't do it by going to war. We went to England and convinced them that they should let us be a country, and so we worked with them."²
>
> —Stuart McNish, host of *Conversations That Matter*

Canada's provinces also have governing powers. The provincial governments, composed of elected representatives, enact laws governing education, health care, and road regulations for their own provinces. For instance, provinces decide what types of schools are available for young people to attend. They also set the legal age at which teens can begin working as well as the minimum wages they can expect to be paid. In addition, provincial governments determine the age at which teens can drop out of school, sign contracts, drive, and purchase alcohol or cigarettes.

Eighteen is considered the age of majority in Canada. Canadians can vote once they turn eighteen, the same age at which they will be treated as adults in criminal court. If their parents do

> "This country is made up of multiple different people from various different ethnic groups and backgrounds and working together to have a constitutional ... democracy, to have a land of freedom and opportunity—that's really the promise of Canada."[3]
>
> —Daniel Sims, a history professor at the University of Alberta

not object, sixteen-year-olds can join the military but cannot be sent into dangerous situations until they reach eighteen.

Canada's body of laws dates back to 1763. These laws were created under British rule and observed as Canadian law even after the country won its independence. However, in 1982 Canadian lawmakers drafted the country's first constitution, adopting many of the laws that had been in existence since the eighteenth century. Included in the constitution is the Canadian Charter of Rights and Freedoms—a body of laws similar to the US Bill of Rights. The charter guarantees all citizens freedom to practice their religion, peacefully assemble, hold opinions, and benefit from a free press. The charter also specifies that both English and French are the country's official languages and that students have the right to be educated in either language. This right is especially important to French-speaking Canadians, who make up a much smaller percentage of the population than English speakers.

As Canada celebrated its 150th birthday in 2017, the country has continued to be a beacon for immigrants. According to Daniel Sims, a history professor at the University of Alberta in Augustana,

> This country is made up of multiple different people from various different ethnic groups and backgrounds and working together to have a constitutional monarchy or [parliamentary] democracy, to have a land of freedom and opportunity—that's really the promise of Canada. That's why we still have immigrants coming to Canada, this promise that if they come to Canada they'll be able to live free and be able to live life as they see fit.[3]

A Nation of Immigrants

Proof of Canada's desire to open its borders to diverse peoples can be found in its population statistics. One in five people living in the country—or, about 7 million people—are immigrants. One immigrant who found a new home in Canada is Vancouver resident Tima Kurdi, who emigrated from Syria to be with her Canadian husband. Kurdi's initial impression was that Canada reminded her of her homeland where, years before the outbreak of her country's 2011 civil war, Christians, Jews, and Muslims lived together peacefully. Since the outbreak of the war, Canada has agreed to take in twenty-five thousand Syrian refugees caught up in the fighting. "In Canada, we are showing the world," she says. "The majority of Canadians have opened their hearts

Queen Elizabeth's Role in Canada

Although Canada gained its independence from Great Britain in 1867, Canada remains a member of the British Commonwealth—a voluntary association of Great Britain and fifty-two former British colonies established to maintain British culture and values. As a member of the British Commonwealth, Canada recognizes the sovereignty of the British royal family.

Therefore, even though she makes her home in Great Britain, Queen Elizabeth II or one of her representatives remains a considerable presence in Canada. Canadian money bears her likeness and, indeed, the queen has taken more trips to Canada than she has to any other country in the world. Likewise, Canadians who travel do so with passports granted to them by the queen.

When someone swears an oath in Canada, he or she is likely to do so in the queen's name. Police officers, legislators, public servants, and military recruits are all asked to swear allegiance to her. She also lends her name and the weight of her title to Canadian charities such as the Red Cross, the Humane Association, and the Cancer Society.

And although the queen is largely regarded as a ceremonial figure with no constitutional authority to govern, she does maintain some powers under law. The queen has the power to pardon any Canadian citizen she chooses—for any offense—and to grant immunity to anyone she chooses. That means she can decide that someone should not be charged with a crime; nonetheless, she rarely exercises this power.

> "The majority of Canadians have opened their hearts to the [Syrian] refugees. Here you are allowed to keep your culture and still be Canadian."[4]
>
> —Tima Kurdi of Vancouver, who emigrated from Syria

to the refugees. Here you are allowed to keep your culture and still be Canadian."[4]

These immigrants—not only from Syria but other lands as well—have brought their lifestyles and traditions. In Canada it is possible to hear Spanish, Italian, Vietnamese, Hindi, Chinese, and other languages spoken in immigrant neighborhoods. In Vancouver, where Kurdi lives, there are many wealthy immigrants from China. One such immigrant is Weymi Cho, whose family sent her to boarding school in Vancouver at age fourteen. Although she speaks English, Cho and her friends prefer to converse in Mandarin. Cho's family and many similarly wealthy families choose Vancouver as a destination for their children because of its warm climate and good schools.

Religious Diversity

Although many languages are spoken, English and French are, nevertheless, the country's official languages, and it is those two languages that are heard most often. Indeed, the Canadian government requires all signs to be written in both English and French.

According to the government agency Statistics Canada, which is the equivalent to the US Census Bureau, 5.8 million Canadians are capable of conducting conversations in both English and French. That means 17.5 percent of Canadians are bilingual. The number of bilingual Canadians is highest in Quebec, where 42 percent of Canadians are fluent in both languages. However, the French influence remains predominant in Quebec, where French is the province's official language. Therefore, teenagers from Quebec might speak French at home and also attend French immersion schools.

In addition to living amid differing cultures and languages, Canadian teens also find themselves living in the midst of a religiously diverse nation, a result of their country's policy of welcoming outsiders. During the colonial era, the Catholic French and Protestant British established their faiths, converting the indigenous peoples to Christianity. Today less than 1 percent of the population practices First Nation religious customs that involve the celebration of animal spirits and a beneficent creator.

But with immigrants accounting for one out of every five people living in the country, there is a growing presence for other religions too. Muslims, Sikhs, Hindus, and Buddhists now make up about 7 percent of the population, but their numbers are expected to grow in the future as more people of those faiths make Canada their home. A 2015 poll conducted by the Angus Reid Institute, a Canadian polling organization, reported that since 1971 the number of Muslims in the country had climbed 700 percent; Hindus, 650 percent; Sikhs, 367 percent; and Buddhists, 1,000 percent.

A Syrian refugee prepares refreshments for visitors. She and her family are among the thousands of Syrians who have fled the violence in their country and found refuge and welcome in Canada.

Born in Pakistan, sixteen-year-old Maryann Wajahat, whose family practices Islam, now lives in Saskatoon, Saskatchewan. She says,

> Living in Saskatoon, you don't have that many Muslims around you, because it's not that big of a population. I can guarantee every Muslim's friends are more than 50 percent white. We don't stick in little groups—over here, everyone's spread out. I know there's always going to be people who are ignorant or hard-headed and are not going to want to open their minds to new ideas. That's totally understandable. But I know that the majority are welcoming and open, and that really helps reassure me that Canada is still diverse. I know that diversity is always going to be there.[5]

Canadian English

Although Canada has been heavily influenced by Great Britain, France, and America, it is also a unique country in its own right—and that includes having some words and expressions that are found nowhere else. Canada also has its own dictionary (the *Canadian Oxford Dictionary*) that is unlike dictionaries found in the United States or Britain. Katherine Barber, a former editor of the Canadian dictionary, wrote the book *Only in Canada, You Say: A Treasury of Canadian Language,* which discusses these unique expressions.

Known as "Canada's Word Lady," Barber collected more than one thousand expressions unique to Canadians. For example, to come *from away* means someone is not a resident of Atlantic Canada. A *hoser* refers to a person who is acting like a fool. Students who *write a test* are taking a test. One puts on shoes called *runners* to participate in gym class.

Some of the expressions Barber mentions in her book are drawn from the Canadian national pastime of hockey. For instance, if one *deks* an opposing player, he or she knocks them down, and if they *stickhandle* a problem, they have expertly solved it.

But twelve-year-old Ameera Khan, a Muslim girl living in Surrey, British Columbia, admits to having a harder time. Ameera explains,

> My friends from school are from all different backgrounds, but most of them celebrate Halloween and Christmas. Sometimes they look at me weird when I say I don't do that. I try to tell all my friends about [the Muslim holidays] Eid and Ramadan, but you kind of have to repeat it a lot or they forget. Sometimes, it's harder for me, because kids will say, "I'm a Christian," and everyone else is like, "Oh, you're Christian! Cool!" But then I say, "I'm Muslim," and some people are like, "Ohhh, you're Muslim. Oh." I don't really like being judged by what I believe in.[6]

Ameera's difficulty in finding acceptance is understandable. The Canadian government and other national institutions may have adopted a policy to embrace immigrants, but individuals are, nevertheless, free to harbor their own beliefs. If individual Canadians do not feel they need to welcome immigrants, then that means the Canadian government has more work to do to spread the message that Canada is a country that welcomes outsiders. It is a policy that has made Canada into a nation that believes diversity is a strength—an attitude that has prevailed for generations as the French- and English-speaking Canadians have learned to put their differences aside and live together as a united people.

CHAPTER TWO

Families in Transition

The Canadian family is in transition, no longer reflecting the common notion of the traditional family: a household led by a working husband and a wife who stays home to raise the children. During the 1960s more than 90 percent of Canadian families fell under that description. Today that type of family is less common. According to Statistics Canada, just 67 percent of Canadian families are headed by husbands and wives. It has become common in recent years to find families in Canada headed by single parents, couples living together out of wedlock, or same-sex couples. Beginning in the mid-1980s researchers noticed "rapid change in Canadian families, with a trend towards increasing diversity of family structures," says a study issued by the Ontario Human Rights Commission. "The 'traditional' family consisting of a father in the paid labour force, married to a woman who is a full-time caregiver for their children, is only one of a wide variety of family types."[7]

Moreover, it is common in Canada to find families living under the same roofs consisting of more than just mothers, fathers, sons, and daughters. Grandparents, uncles and aunts, cousins, and other members of extended families may be part of everyday life in the typical Canadian home. In prior years, an unmarried uncle or aunt may have lived alone. A grandparent who lost a spouse may have also lived alone. Now, according to Statistics Canada, it is not unusual to find extended family members living together, sharing the same roof and the same chores, such as cooking, cleaning, and picking up grandchildren or nieces and nephews from school. According to Statistics Canada, in the 1960s just 8 percent of households included a member of an extended family. Today that number has more than doubled to 17 percent.

A typical example of an extended family sharing the same residence in Canada can be found in the Toronto home of Sunana and David Worts. The Wortses share their home with their daughter Genevieve Metropolis and her husband; the Metropolis's four-year-old son, Oliver; and Oliver's aunt Rebecca. Metropolis says she and her husband moved in with her parents shortly after they were married. The Metropolises were burdened with high bills due to student debt and could not afford a home of their own. Three years later their son, Oliver, was born. Now that Oliver is four and his parents are on a firmer financial footing, the Metropolis family has decided to stay. "We have sit-down meals most nights and Ollie does little projects with every member of the household, from planting mustard seeds with Sunana to drawing with Aunt Rebecca,"[8] says Metropolis.

> "The 'traditional' family consisting of a father in the paid labour force, married to a woman who is a full-time caregiver for their children, is only one of a wide variety of family types."[7]
>
> —Ontario Human Rights Commission

Family Day

The fact that many Canadians welcome members of extended families to move into their homes illustrates how much Canadians value family life. In fact, the provinces of Alberta, Ontario, Saskatchewan, British Columbia, and New Brunswick have declared a specific Monday in February as Family Day, setting aside one day a year to celebrate the value of family life. To encourage families to spend the day together, the provincial governments close schools, and most businesses give their employees the day off as well. Popular Family Day activities include playing games, visiting museums, watching movies, and completing crafting projects together.

Each year on Family Day the Alberta community of St. Albert holds its annual Fire and Ice Festival in Lacombe Lake Park. Attended by some four thousand family members, the festival consists of a number of family-oriented activities, such as an obstacle course, tug-of-war, and campfire. As entertainment, performers juggle flaming torches. And since it is February, Lacombe Lake is frozen, enabling participants to play shinny—an informal hockey match also known as pond hockey. "This is about everybody having a good time," says Bryan Mroz, an official with the St. Albert firefighters' union, which organizes the Fire and Ice Festival. "It's free and fun, so everybody can come out."[9]

In many Canadian communities, shinny is a typical family activity—the game was played by parents and their children long before cities started organizing Family Day events. As a young girl, Catherine Dubois, a teenager who lives in Quebec City, Quebec, watched as her father and brothers played pond hockey. She begged to join them. "I wanted to be like them, and they

A Toronto man and his six-year-old daughter enjoy a toboggan ride on Family Day. On this day each year parents, children, and other relatives gather to celebrate the importance of family.

were playing hockey, so I asked my parents if I could play hockey, too,"[10] she says. Eventually, Dubois joined Canada's National Women's Under-18 Team, and in 2013 she scored a key goal against the US team to win the Women's World Championship in Finland.

Blended Families

Many of the young participants who attend Family Day activities do so with one parent only. Despite the desire of Canadians to make their families work, divorce is common in Canada. According to Statistics Canada, 16 percent of Canadian families are headed by single parents—double the rate found in 1961. When it comes to their parents' divorces, young people in Canada are similar to young people everywhere: They may feel troubled as they face the question of what went wrong in their families. One fifteen-year-old Canadian girl says, "A few years ago my parents split up. It was unexpected and I was devastated. Now I hardly see my dad and when I do it's always for a short period of time. A lot of times I think about what my life would be like if my parents got back together. I have lost focus in school and my grades are slipping. I don't feel like hanging out with my friends anymore or even doing fun social activities."[11]

But divorce can also give parents second chances, and statistics indicate that many Canadians who go through divorce go on to remarry. According to Statistics Canada, 13 percent of Canadian families are regarded as blended families, which means they feature fathers and mothers helping raise each other's children from previous marriages. "We know that families have been blending for a long time," says Nora Spinks, chief executive officer of the Vanier Institute of the Family in Ottawa, Ontario. "As divorce rates go up, it is anticipated there will be a corresponding increase in the number of stepfamilies because by and large as some of the other numbers show, adults in Canada tend to partner. . . . This does help people who are going through [divorce] to feel less alone."[12]

Sometimes a man without children of his own marries a woman with children and suddenly becomes a stepfather. And, certainly, some women find themselves in similar situations. These families are known as simple stepfamilies. According to Statistics Canada, they make up about 7 percent of all blended families.

Therefore, it is much more common for fathers and mothers, both with children of their own, to form new—and sometimes very large—blended families. (These are known as complex stepfamilies.) When Jennifer and Scott Lawson of Grimsby, Ontario, married, they found themselves the parents and stepparents of nine children, ages twenty months to twenty years. Now each parent devotes much of his or her free time to looking after the needs of their children: ranging from feeding and bathing the youngest members to attending school activities for the older children. "When you're getting together with a blended family . . . you have work challenges, you have personal challenges," says Jennifer. "You don't realize that all those little things can make things like blended families even more difficult."[13]

Whether they live in blended families or traditional ones, many Canadian parents attempt to share meals with their children. A poll by the public-opinion tracking company Gallup found that 40 percent of Canadian families make it a point to share evening meals seven nights a week. (In contrast, the poll found that some 28 percent of American families share meals seven nights a week.) Moreover, a study by McGill University in Montreal reported that young Canadians benefit by sharing their meals with their parents and other family members. "The effect doesn't plateau after three or four dinners a week," says study coauthor Frank Elgar, an associate professor of psychiatry at McGill. "The more dinners a week the better."[14]

Rural Life

Although many young Canadians find mealtime to be a regular part of home life, for most teens home is also a place where they take off their shoes at the door, invite their friends over, do their homework, help out with chores, and relax after a busy day at school. At home, teenagers are afforded private spaces, with many parents letting their children have their own rooms if space is available. But some Canadian parents do not allow their teenagers to have their own rooms even though they have the space to give them one. These parents may opt for their children to share rooms in the hope that the siblings will grow to be closer. Sometimes, however, a parent's good intentions on room sharing can backfire. "Some siblings are more like oil and water . . . and

Same-Sex Parenting

In Canada, where same-sex marriage has been legal since 2005, there are 64,576 same-sex couples who are either married or in common-law relationships, according to Statistics Canada. Living with those couples are some ninety-six hundred children.

One of those couples is Nathan and John. They have been married for about six years and have adopted Brynn and Emery, two young girls who are sisters. The girls refer to Nathan as "Daddy," and John is called "Dad." Nathan, twenty-seven, and John, twenty-four, are raising the girls in the same small town in which they grew up: North Bay, Ontario. North Bay has only fifty thousand residents, and its main industries are mining and the military. According to Nathan and John, people of North Bay fully accept their family. Says Nathan,

> We are so overjoyed to have partaken in this crazy adventure of parenting. It is the most rewarding thing we have ever done.... John and I both have large families so we truly understand how much of a blessing family really is. For us as Canadians, the thought and process of adoption seemed so obvious for us. It is such a common thing here in Canada to see same-sex parents.

Quoted in *Huffington Post*, "A Young Gay Dad Family in Small-Town Canada," February 23, 2017. www.huffingtonpost.com.

---

the more time they spend together, it can create more problems and they just don't find their way out of it,"[15] says Alyson Schafer, a Toronto-based psychotherapist.

Most people in Canada live in or near big cities; according to Statistics Canada, 81 percent of Canadians live in cities or their suburbs. (In fact, a third of all Canadians live in the country's three largest cities: Toronto, Montreal, and Vancouver.) That means just 19 percent of Canadians live in rural regions or small towns. Young people in rural Canada often live on farms or ranches near sparsely populated small towns. They are expected to help plant crops, drive tractors, and operate other farm machines. Their other chores may include helping milk the cows, feed the animals, tend the horses, and perform other chores to assist their parents. Many small towns in rural Canada are so small that they may lack a post office, school, and grocery store.

A young girl gets an early introduction to feeding the family's cows. Young people who grow up on farms and ranches in Canada often help their parents with chores, including planting crops, driving tractors, milking cows, and feeding livestock.

Young people who live in rural towns are more likely to have mothers who do not work outside the home. They know and feel connected to their neighbors and never have to worry about losing their front door key because few rural residents lock them.

Indeed, many young Canadians hope they never have to move to cities—preferring to live their whole lives on their farms or ranches or in small towns. "I don't like the city too much. It's too crowded, it's noisy," says Greg Dawson, who lived on a cattle ranch near the Alberta town of Nanton in his teens. "You can escape from the noise out here."[16] John Gale also lived on a ranch in Alberta in his teens. The ranch was located near Cochrane, a town about 30 miles (48 km) north of the city of Calgary. When he was growing up there, Cochrane had a population of ten thousand—and even that was too large for his tastes. "There's too many people in town," he told an interviewer when he was fifteen. After graduation from high school, his plan was to work as a farrier—a craftsman who trims the hooves of horses and shoes the animals as well. "I've lived here most of my life, and I want to stay here."[17]

One reason many teenagers prefer life in small towns or on their ranches or farms is the lack of crime in rural Canada. "It's much safer here than in the cities," Nadine Sigvaldason told an interviewer when she was a sixteen-year-old high school student living in Arborg, Manitoba, a town with a current population of about twelve hundred. "You can send your kids out trick-or-treating and it's safe."[18] And Nadine's classmate, Jennifer Blandford, told the same interviewer that she recalled seeing a bicycle left outside a nearby store for many months. She said, "There was like a bike left outside . . . in, like, May, and it's still there."[19]

> "I don't like the city too much. It's too crowded, it's noisy."[16]
>
> —Greg Dawson, who grew up on a ranch in Alberta

City Life

Many teens who live in or near small towns may enjoy all that rural life in Canada has to offer, but many urban teens would not think of trading places with them. Big cities like Toronto, Montreal, and Vancouver offer opportunities for entertainment, education, and connecting with people that simply are not available in rural Canada.

Young people in Toronto can attend the YouTube FanFest, an annual bash in which popular YouTube performers gather for live performances of the acts they have posted on the Internet streaming site. Toronto also hosts the iHeartRadio Much Music Video Awards, which are attended by many of the country's top recording stars. Many young Toronto fans line the red carpet for glimpses of their favorite artists. Big cities in Canada are also home to some of the country's most important universities—places where many young Canadians aspire to attend. Among these schools are McGill University, the University of British Columbia in Vancouver, York University in Toronto, and the University of Ottawa.

A group of boys in Calgary show off their skateboard tricks. Canadian youth who grow up in the cities find many ways to entertain themselves.

Indeed, some young people who have spent their lives in small Canadian towns wonder what life would be like in big cities. Many want to do things with their lives other than work on farms and realize that moving to big cities may be the only opportunity they have for achieving their goals. When Kim Andrei was eighteen, she had lived her whole life on a farm near Ogema, Saskatchewan—a town with a population of about four hundred residents. She realized her opportunities in Ogema were limited. After high school, she planned to move to Winnipeg to pursue a new life. "If you actually put yourself to something, you can find something to do for the rest of your life," she told a reporter. "And I think you have to be in a big area to do that."[20] Added Ogema resident Lindsay

Bacon, who was sixteen at the time, "We don't get to interact with other cultures and that's something you're going to need when you get out [of Ogema]."[21]

Typical Teenagers

Some experts warn that small towns in Canada often offer young people few positive activities to fill their time, such as extracurricular activities at school, organizations that can use their help as volunteers, or places where they can find after-school jobs. Toronto pediatrician Miriam Kaufman, who is regarded as an expert on adolescent sexuality, observes that Canadian parents who choose rural areas to raise their children may be fooled into thinking they are more safe and nurturing. "People move to rural areas

Sugar Shacks

From early March to early May, teenagers in Quebec, along with their parents and grandparents, may gather together at restaurants known as sugar shacks to enjoy meals drenched in maple syrup and history. Located near where the maple trees are producing sap that will be boiled into maple syrup, sugar shacks may be plain or fancy and typically serve a menu that is similar to what the men and women who tapped the trees hundreds of years ago used to eat to keep their energy up. It has been estimated that there are two hundred sugar shacks scattered across Quebec where families can chow down on pea soup, assorted meats, pancakes, and maple syrup that is poured on top of snow and scraped off and eaten with Popsicle sticks.

Marie Asselin, a resident of Quebec City who blogs about food, recalls,

When I was growing up, visiting a sugar shack in March was a tradition. It was the quintessential Québécois family activity. It seemed as though everyone knew someone in his or her close or extended families who had a sugar shack, so we would all go and spend a sunny weekend day there, running among the maple trees, dipping our fingers in the maple sap (which was at the time still collected in buckets—at least at the farm I remember visiting), and eating as much maple taffy as possible.

Marie Asselin, "Brunch at the Sugar Shack," *Food Nouveau* (blog), March 12, 2015. http://foodnouveau.com.

because it's a better place to raise their children. And that may be true but once you hit adolescence, there's not much to do in smaller centres beyond drink and have sex."[22]

Still, Canada is a modern country, and young people have widespread access to the Internet, social media, and television. The media have helped connect urban teens to rural teens, erasing many of the differences in how they perceive one another.

That is the conclusion drawn by Reginald Bibby, a sociologist at the University of Lethbridge in Alberta who conducted a recent Project Teen Canada survey. He says, "Growing access to media in its diverse forms—and particularly television and the Internet—increasingly has eroded geographical boundaries. Consequently, young people look pretty much the same."[23]

In other words, Canadian teenagers are, at their core, typical teenagers—whether they grow up in big cities such as Toronto or Vancouver or in small towns such as Flin Flon, Manitoba; or Mahone Bay, Nova Scotia. Regardless of where they call home, these young people are likely to be members of close-knit families. Many invite grandparents and other extended family members to move in. And if their marriages do not work, many Canadian parents are willing to try again, forming blended families. Canadian family members enjoy spending their time together—often finding a frozen lake for a vigorous game of shinny.

CHAPTER THREE

Education and Work

With a literacy rate of 97 percent, there is no mistaking that education is highly valued in Canada, and Canadian students excel when compared to students from other countries. In fact, in a recent international assessment test, fifteen-year-old Canadians placed seventh out of forty-four countries in math, science, and reading proficiency.

Their performances in those subjects scored better than students from the United States, Great Britain, Australia, and Finland but not quite as good as teens from the math and science powerhouses of Korea and Singapore. In interpreting the 2012 survey results, Jeff Johnson, Alberta's education minister, said, "The report also confirms that Canadian 15-year-olds who do well in problem solving also tend to do well in the core subject areas, suggesting that how mathematics, reading and science are taught in Canadian classrooms prepare students well to solve real-life challenges."[24] Ultimately those challenges include deciding what careers they will train for and whether they will attend trade schools or universities after they graduate from high school.

When Alexander Deans, now nineteen, was in high school, he began using his science education to solve real-life problems. As an eleventh-grade student at the Académie Ste-Cécile International School in Windsor, Ontario, Alexander sought a patent on a device he created after watching a woman with poor vision have trouble crossing the street. He says, "I went up to her and asked if she needed any help and I realized she was visually impaired. I saw that she didn't have any independence and couldn't navigate well. . . . The best part of science is using it to make other people's lives better."[25] Alexander came up with a digital tool with sensors that could act like another pair of eyes for the visually impaired.

The Canadian School Year

Young people like Alexander are dedicated students who make the most of what Canadian schools have to offer. Nonetheless, some students are underachievers—despite the government's efforts to make sure all students attend school and receive quality educations. In fact, not showing up for school can have serious consequences, as one sixteen-year-old girl from Barrie, Ontario, found out. The girl spent a night in jail in 2016 after habitually missing school and then failing to show up in court to answer for her behavior. The province's Education Act makes it mandatory for all students to attend school and empowers police to arrest and jail offenders.

Canadian law requires students to attend school for twelve years, from age six to eighteen. The federal government lets each province run its own schools and decide what students will learn in each grade. Students do not have to attend kindergarten, but those who do begin their educations at age four or five. Canada's youngest students, from grade one through grade seven, attend elementary school and then move on to middle school for grades eight and nine. High school includes students in the tenth through twelfth grades. Rarely are students forced to repeat grades; usually, a student must repeat a grade when he or she misses too many school days due to illness.

The school year runs from September to June, with students having summers off; the typical school day begins around 8:00 or 9:00 a.m. and typically ends at 2:30 or 3:30 p.m. Students who live too far away to walk to school are transported by school buses to get to classes. For those who wish to attend private schools far from their home, this may involve spending several hours a day on school buses.

Canadian students can pick among many different types of schools. Public schools are available as well as private schools. In Canada, the Catholic Church also operates schools. Other Canadian Christians can attend so-called separate schools, which are operated in accordance with the principles of Protestant denominations.

The Canadian School Day

Selection of a school is, of course, a very personal choice, often made by parents based on their children's needs and the quality

Ninth graders in Toronto work on class assignments. High student test scores and a 97 percent literacy rate among the total population reflect the value Canadians place on education.

of the school where they wish to enroll their sons and daughters. Certainly, most young people in Canada do attend public schools. According to Statistics Canada, there are more than 5 million students in all grade levels attending public schools. However, many Canadians are very particular about where they send their children. School quality is so important to Canadian families that many parents choose the neighborhoods in which to live based on the quality of the local schools.

Regardless of where young people attend school, their teachers are likely to keep them very busy. Public school student Jackie Allen attends the sixth grade in Halifax, Nova Scotia. She rises at 7:00 a.m., and after a breakfast of her favorite cold cereal,

Homeschooling in Canada

Many students are homeschooled in Canada, meaning they are taught by their parents. In recent years the number of homeschooled students has been rising as more parents choose this option. According to a study by the Fraser Institute, a Vancouver-based organization that studies public policy issues, some twenty-one thousand Canadian students were homeschooled in 2012, the last year for which statistics are available. According to the Fraser Institute, that number represents a 29 percent rise over the number of homeschooled students reported in 2006. Deani Van Pelt, a senior fellow at the institute and the author of the study, says,

> It's worth asking, first of all, why families are increasingly choosing this option. A few decades ago, the main drivers were ideology and religion—meaning that families wanted their education to better reflect their beliefs. Not so much anymore. A recent review of the research found that families are choosing homeschooling for practical reasons. It just fits the way some families live and raise their children nowadays.

For Caitlin, who attended public school through sixth grade, homeschooling was just a better fit for her and allowed her to more fully reach her potential. She says, "I became a more self-confident person—learned to figure out how to get what I wanted without necessarily following the conventional path. . . . I was able to have many experiences that would not have been possible if I spent most of my days in school."

Deani Van Pelt, "Home-Schooling on the Rise in Canada," Fraser Institute, 2015. www.fraserinstitute.org.

Quoted in Sue Patterson, *Homeschooled Teens: 75 Young People Speak About Their Lives Without School.* Wimberley, TX: 2nd Tier, 2015, p. 41.

Shreddies, she walks to elementary school with her friends. Because Canada has two official languages, English and French, Jackie's morning frequently involves creative writing in English as well as lessons in French, which she has been studying for two years. Other subjects include art, math, science, social studies, and gym. At midday, Jackie goes home for lunch. Usually, she eats a sandwich for lunch—often grilled cheese.

She has to return to school within an hour. One day a week she has a violin lesson at school instead of going home for lunch. Afternoons in school focus on a variety of activities, among them a Canadian version of kickball. She says,

On Wednesdays and Fridays, we do Book Buddies. Older kids are paired with younger kids. We help them read, write and do math. On Fridays, we sometimes play soccer-baseball in the gym. It's a game that is soccer and baseball mixed together. There's an infield with four bases: first, second, third and home. A pitcher rolls the ball to you, and you have to kick it and try to get a home run.[26]

Jackie finishes her school day at about 3:00 p.m. She spends about twenty minutes on homework each night, watches some television, and heads to bed at 8:30 p.m.

Preparing for the Next Level of Schooling
Once students like Jackie reach high school, they will be faced with required courses in a variety subjects. These courses usually consist of English, French, social studies, algebra, geometry, and calculus. Teens who do not want to go to a university can choose vocational courses that can place them on the path to perhaps take over the family farm, learn to be a caregiver for children or the elderly, develop business skills needed in an office, or go into the building trades.

They receive grades for each course based on their performance on tests, homework, projects, and class participation. Students who want to go to a university in Canada do not need to take special standardized tests such as the SAT or ACT—their high school transcripts suffice. However, if Canadian teens desire to attend a university in America, they do need to take the SAT or ACT.

Although preparing for their future is the main goal of Canadian teenagers in high school, their school lives are not just about studying. Extracurricular activities such as participation in band, choir, drama clubs, and sports teams, including baseball, hockey, and soccer, are important. These activities help them make friends, help them develop leadership skills, and make them more attractive candidates to college admission officers as well as to prospective employers.

Busy Lives Lead to Pressure
These activities are designed to help Canadian teenagers succeed. Certainly, young people in Canada often feel the pressure

to succeed. In fact, one study found that they are working harder than teenagers from America, Australia, Great Britain, Norway, and France. According to the Statistics Canada study, between schoolwork, family chores, and part-time jobs, teens put in fifty-hour workweeks, and that pace leads to stress. As a result, 64 percent of teenagers surveyed said they sacrifice sleep to get more accomplished, and 34 percent said they feel compelled to take on more than they believe they could reasonably accomplish. "When I had a [part-time] job I was a complete workaholic, and at school, I'm a perfectionist. So I would get stressed out all the time," says Brianne Daigle, seventeen, of Toronto. "Then you get sick because you're stressed. It's a terrible circle."[27]

Many young Canadians, such as this cashier at an Ikea store in British Columbia, fill their days with school, chores, and part-time jobs. Trying to squeeze so many activities into their days can be stressful.

Some of the stress teens experience is the result of having to decide what career path to take, a decision they need to begin thinking about while still in high school. A recent study by polling company Ipsos Reid asked more than eight hundred Canadian high school students about their future plans. In the survey, about 20 percent of the students said they did not know what they would do after high school, and more than half of those who were undecided reported feeling stress over their pending decisions. Nearly half of students polled also worried about finding time to do homework, work part-time, participate in after-school activities, complete chores, and whether they would have enough money to afford more education after high school.

> "When I had a [part-time] job I was a complete workaholic, and at school, I'm a perfectionist. So I would get stressed out all the time."[27]
>
> —Student Brianne Daigle, seventeen, of Toronto

Students who had already made up their minds favored having a science-related career (39 percent), the most popular category. Of the others expressing a preference, 13 percent were interested in art, 12 percent in pursuing a trade, 9 percent in business, and 3 percent in music. Regardless of what they might want to study, teens are thoughtful about what they would look for in a future career. According to Canada 2067, the website of a group promoting careers in math, science, technology, and engineering, more than 70 percent of thirteen- to seventeen-year-old Canadians want to help people, make a contribution, solve problems, and have the authority to make decisions. Slightly less than 50 percent of the 818 teens surveyed said they would like to own their own businesses.

Universities and Trade Preparation Colleges

Many teens face pressure and competition to win admission to postsecondary programs. The Ipsos Reid poll found that 63 percent of high school students surveyed were worried about getting into colleges or universities. Among their fears were that their grades were not high enough or their extracurricular activities were not strong enough to earn a place in their chosen field. In addition, some students who have done extremely well in high school worry that they may not be able to maintain their high grades in the future. Such a fate nearly undid Scott Penner as an engineering student at the University of Manitoba. Penner had excelled in high school math and science, but at the university he was stunned to receive fewer As and to fail calculus. "It was a bit of a shock,"[28] he says. Penner redoubled his efforts and was able to pass calculus the second time.

In Canada there is a marked difference between colleges and universities. Universities are academic institutions that confer bachelor's, master's, and doctoral degrees. Earning a bachelor's degree, for example, takes at least three years, with an optional fourth year for those who want to take honors classes. Colleges, on the other hand, provide students with hands-on instruction. Sometimes the instruction is in a trade such as mechanical repair, construction, food services, or farming. Sometimes it is in business, computer science, visual arts, engineering, and child care. Depending on the college and course work required, college certificates can be obtained in as little as eight months or as long as two years. Colleges may offer apprenticeship programs and award pupils with certificates or diplomas. Usually paired with classroom education, apprenticeships let students earn money as they master on-the-job skills. Training to be an electrician or a plumber, for example, typically includes an apprenticeship.

> "It's like, impossible to get into an electrical company. It's like literally impossible."[29]
>
> —Chris Mazur, an apprentice electrician

Getting into an apprenticeship program can be difficult, a lesson learned by Chris Mazur, twenty-three, of Ottawa. It took him four years to find a slot as an apprentice electrician, during which time he worked three jobs and constantly filled out applications. The problem he encountered is that there are more applicants for electrical apprenticeships than openings. "It's like, impossible to get into an electrical company. It's like literally impossible,"[29] he says. Mazur is receiving his on-the-job training at an electrical contracting company in Ottawa and classroom education at the Ontario College of Trades. Luckily for Mazur, his persistence paid off; if all goes well, he will eventually become a licensed journeyman

French Immersion Schools

Many Canadian students study French in English-speaking public schools, but some teens enroll in schools where French predominates. According to Canadian Parents for French, an organization promoting French education, more than 30 percent of students in most provinces enroll in French immersion schools.

Bryan, who attends the Elmlea French Immersion Junior School in Toronto, believes that his education will make it easier for him to be employed after graduation. He says, "Let's say you want a job but they only have one place. If there's another person who only speaks English but you speak English and French, they'll give you the job because you know more languages."

His fellow student, Ammar, enjoys knowing how to speak French because it provides him with an opportunity to share secrets with his French-speaking brother that their parents, who do not speak French, will not understand. He says, "Sometimes me and my brother will be talking and we don't want Mom to listen, so we just start talking in French."

Although many students like Ammar and Bryan start out in French immersion schools, few actually complete their educations in these schools. In fact, just one out of every four students who start out in French schools makes it all the way through to graduation without switching to an English-speaking school.

Quoted in Tim Johnson, "A Look at French Immersion," *Canadian Family*. www.canadianfamily.ca.

electrician making forty Canadian dollars (about twenty-nine US dollars) an hour.

Where teens live correlates to what they decide to study, especially since each province has its own postsecondary institutions of higher learning. For example, teens who live in rural regions of Alberta, Saskatchewan, and the Yukon account for 21 percent of registered apprenticeship certificates. Trade education is also popular in Quebec, Newfoundland and Labrador, and Nova Scotia. In turn, teens in more metropolitan areas are more likely to opt for a university education. Certain provinces and territories, however, are notable for having the most adults with no education beyond high school: Nunavut, the Northwest Territories, and Newfoundland and Labrador.

Finding Good Jobs

Although Canadians with more education find more opportunities for higher-paying jobs, there are certainly jobs available for high school graduates. Canadian teens who worked while in high school—during the school year or just over the summer—can use experiences they gained to find full-time jobs once high school is over. Jobs they can find immediately after high school include working as retail store clerks, delivery drivers, farmers, secretaries, miners, and oil field workers. Thirteen percent of fifteen- to twenty-four-year-old Canadians are unemployed, a figure that is less than youth unemployment in other countries.

Still, finding a first job can be difficult—even for those who are university educated. Although there are no statistics available on them, some Canadian millennials—whose oldest members were born in 1982—live with their parents after completing their university studies while they seek full-time jobs that pay well enough to live on their own. Among those who are struggling to get their career footing is Clair Parker, who attended Carleton University in Ottawa, where she earned a degree in political science in 2014. Unable to land a job that matched her major, which taught her how government works, the only position she could find was a job as a waitress. "When I came out of university, I wondered, 'Why did I just do that?'" she says. Convinced that her university education had not prepared her for a career, Parker hopes to retrain for a new career in the food industry. This time she plans to enroll in a college to study restaurant marketing. "I just hope I come out actually employable,"[30] she says.

> "When I came out of university, I wondered, 'Why did I just do that?'"[30]
>
> —Clair Parker, a Carleton University graduate

Canadian Business, a magazine produced by the Canadian Chamber of Commerce, points out that millennials currently make up the largest share of the Canadian workforce. Millennials who have the easiest time finding jobs are those who study one of the ten fields identified by the Internet career site CareerCast. Many of the jobs in these fields involve computers, such as data scientist, market research analyst, social media manager, and computer systems analyst.

A young waitress serves seafood at a restaurant in Quebec. Some young Canadians have found it difficult to find jobs in their chosen fields after graduating from a university.

Young people between fifteen and twenty-four who are seeking employment can get free career advice, résumé help, and counseling at Canadian youth centers run by provincial governments. In 2017 Calgary held a job fair that drew some five thousand young people looking for employment in a region where the oil industry had shed many jobs. Among them was eighteen-year-old Moyo Adeniren, who had hoped to find a job to give her some extra money as she began her education at the University of Calgary. Adeniren admits that she feels a lot of pressure as she begins looking for employment and wonders whether she will be successful. She says, "I feel like when we're all getting out of university or we're all getting out of high school, there's this chance of 'We're out of school now, we've done what everyone says is the expectation, so now we're going to simply go and get a job.' But there's still people working who should be retired or want to be retired but they can't because they need work. Then there's no job for us. It's not economics, there's just no place for us to be in."[31]

The challenges faced by young people like Chris Mazur, Clair Parker, and Moyo Adeniren illustrate that, essentially, Canadians are no different from young people growing up most everywhere else. Their success depends largely on their dedication to their schoolwork, their ambition, the choices they make about what to study and which careers to pursue, and being in the right place at the right time.

CHAPTER FOUR

Social Life

Hundreds of teenage girls from throughout Canada flocked to Leduc, Alberta, in April 2017 to compete in the annual Canadian Ringette Championships. The players had spent the year competing in local leagues, then earning their places on teams representing their home cities. When the championships finally arrived, the girls were prepared for some very vigorous ringette competitions. One player looking forward to the championships was Alyssa Suchan, a member of the host city Leduc team. "I love the speed and the competition," said Alyssa, who competed in the under sixteen division, in which squads are composed of girls ages fifteen and sixteen. "I hope to grow my game and push myself beyond my potential. It's incredible to have the opportunity to play against the best. Someone on the ice will be better than me and they'll make me want it even more."[32]

Ringette is similar to ice hockey, but there are significant differences. Although played by both boys and girls, the sport is dominated by girls' teams. The roots of the sport trace back to 1963, when Sam Jacks, a recreation director and sports enthusiast from North Bay, Ontario, saw the need for a winter sport that would appeal to girls. The game is played on ice but uses a rubber ring rather than a puck. As with hockey, the object of the game is to bring the ring up the ice and shoot it into the opponent's goal. A key difference between hockey and ringette is that the sticks are straight in ringette, not curved like in hockey. Also, ringette is not a contact sport; players are challenged to

> "It's incredible to have the opportunity to play against the best. Someone on the ice will be better than me and they'll make me want it even more."[32]
>
> —Ringette player Alyssa Suchan

finesse and pass the rubber ring up the ice rather than slamming through opponents as hockey players are trained to do.

Ringette is very popular. According to Ringette Canada, the national governing body for the sport, some thirty thousand young people in Canada play ringette on nearly two thousand local teams. A player on an under nineteen team from Winnipeg, Michaela Kelly, says the sport is special to her because she can compete alongside her twin sister, Claire. "It was a great experience and getting to share that with my sister makes it special," Michaela says. "Some people grow apart from their siblings, but I'm always going to have my sister there."[33]

Hockey Still Dominates

The image of Canadians playing sports on ice—whether the game is hockey or ringette—is certainly familiar to people worldwide. It is hockey, however, that is regarded as the national sport of Canada. Indeed, the National Hockey League is dominated by players from Canada, and it is easy to see why. Hockey Canada, the national governing body for amateur hockey in the country, estimates that more than six hundred thousand young people—including some eighty-seven thousand girls—play the sport on an amateur level.

Hockey takes many physical skills, but the most important one is the ability to skate on ice. Because of Canada's northern location, long winters, and preponderance of frozen ponds, winter sports are popular with Canadian teenagers, and the most popular of those sports involve ice skating. It makes sense that ice skating would catch on in Canada—French explorers knew how to skate, as did many of the British settlers who came to settle the country. Some historians suggest that even before the European colonists arrived in Canada, the First Nation people devised their own ice skates by strapping animal bones to the bottoms of their footwear.

In modern times, it may seem difficult to find a Canadian who does not know how to skate. Recalling his childhood, Winnipeg mayor Brian Bowman says,

> In the winters, we spent a lot of time outside. Some of my fondest memories were playing hockey in the backyard. I

was a Varsity View Falcon, and our local community centre was down the street. It had three sheets of outdoor ice. At the end of the school day, everybody would go home, but as soon as dinner was done, I was back at the rink. . . . We wouldn't even phone our friends. You would just show up at the rink, and that's where all your buddies were. We spent hours freezing our toes and drinking terrible hot chocolate to warm up.[34]

Skating and playing hockey on frozen ponds and lakes are favorite youth activities during Canada's cold winters. Many Canadians have fond memories of hours spent outdoors on the ice.

The Sport of Curling

As Bowman explains, impromptu hockey pickup games among friends are common throughout Canada. But hockey as well as ringette are not the only games played on ice. Another popular sport played by many young people in Canada is curling. Two teams compete against each other to see who can get as many "stones" as close as possible to the center of a bull's-eye that is 150 feet (46 m) away on the ice. The four players on each side wear special shoes made for sliding and gloves to protect their hands from the cold. The person who literally calls the shots for each team is the skip, or captain.

Canadian Football

Although ice hockey dominates Canadian sports on both the professional and amateur levels, Canadian-style football is also very popular. According to School Sport Canada, a national organization that regulates school sports, Canadian football is played by more than nine hundred high school teams.

Canadian football is also played at both the university and professional levels by teams that are members of the Canadian Football League (CFL). Twenty-six percent of Canadians aged eighteen to thirty-four watch CFL games on television, following such teams as the Calgary Stampeders, Edmonton Eskimos, and the Montreal Alouettes.

In Canadian football, the object is the same as in the American version. Players attempt to move the ball up the field, scoring touchdowns. However, there are some significant differences. The Canadian game is played on a larger field, which measures 110 yards (101 m) long and 65 yards (59 m) wide, as opposed to the American version, which is 100 yards (91 m) long and 53.5 yards (49 m) wide. Also, Canadian teams are composed of twelve players instead of eleven under US rules. And Canadians have three downs to gain 10 yards for a first down, but in the American version offenses have four downs to make a first down. Also in the Canadian version, the running backs and receivers can begin running forward before the snap, an action that would draw a penalty in America. "One less down and a longer and wider field make for more daring plays, more gadget plays and more razzle-dazzle," says Canadian sportswriter Randy Russon.

Randy Russon, "Still Crazy About Canadian Football After All These Years," *Sault This Week*, June 27, 2016. www.sault thisweek.com.

The game is played in six to ten innings. A single inning lasts until the players on each side have eight stones down the ice toward the bull's-eye. To deliver a stone, a right-handed player kneels on the ice while gripping the stone's handle in the right hand. The player then glides forward with the right knee bent and left foot extended behind on the ice, before letting go of the stone. Delivering the stone takes finesse because the stones, which resemble tea kettles without spouts, each weigh 40 pounds (18 kg), and the way the team controls where the stone lands is by getting in front of it and sweeping the ice with brooms. The sweeping creates grooves in the ice that control the stone's direction while melting the ice under the stone, allowing it to move faster. Sara England, nineteen, is a member of a curling team that recently competed in the sport's junior championships. She makes it clear that it takes an athlete to play the game competitively. She says, "You can't just walk down the ice and lightly brush a rock. You actually have to put in all the effort in the off-ice training—and the mental training, I would say, is even harder than the physical training."[35]

According to Curling Canada, the governing body that oversees the sport, more than seven hundred thousand Canadians play on amateur curling teams. And unlike hockey, which is dominated by male players, or ringette, which is dominated by female players, curling has wide appeal to both genders: About two-thirds of curlers are male, and one-third are female. Moreover, the largest percentage of curlers, about 18 percent, are under the age of seventeen.

Music and Television

Ice skating and other winter sports dominate the free time of many young Canadians, but it is also true that Canadian teens are very much like teens elsewhere, and that means they like music and television. Because of its proximity to the United States, Canadian teens are familiar with American television and music—although the country has a vibrant music scene and its own television networks.

Canadian teens listen to a lot of music—as many as thirty-one hours a week, according to a report by the global information-gathering company Nielsen. Teens stream music through their smartphones, tablets, and laptops. Dance, hip-hop, and rap music are the most popular choices, Nielsen reported. Many teens enjoy the music of Justin Bieber, Shawn Mendes, Alessia Cara, and Ruth B, all of whom won Canadian Radio Music Awards in 2017. The awards are the Canadian equivalent of the Grammy Awards in America.

Teens spend about twenty-four hours a week watching television, according to a recent survey of young people between the ages of nine and eighteen commissioned by the Shaw Rocket Fund in Alberta. The fund concentrates on developing good media habits among young people. In the survey, half the respondents said they enjoy watching programs made in Canada about Canada, and one of their favorite networks is the homegrown CTV.

The network contains a mix of American-made shows like *Lucifer*, *The Big Bang Theory,* and *Criminal Minds* as well as Canadian shows like *Masterchef Canada* and *Motive*. One of the most popular television shows in Canada for teens is the high school drama *Degrassi: New Class*, part of a series that debuted in 1979. Although the show has featured different so-called classmates over the years, it has stayed fresh by zeroing in on the changing types of controversial issues teens confront in their daily lives. The musical artist Drake, who grew up in Toronto, was one of the original cast members. Writer David Berry explains the show's enduring appeal: "The secret sauce of *Degrassi* . . . was that teens, like most of us, just want to see themselves. It's easy to see teens being teens online, but it's never been reflected in pop culture to a degree that approaches reality."[36]

Social Media and Cyberbullying

A lot of television shows watched by Canadian teens are streamed over the Internet. In fact, the Internet is widely available throughout Canada—even in the most remote regions of the country. When Canada's Center for Digital and Media Literacy conducted a recent classroom survey of fourth- to eleventh-grade students, the organization found that all students had access to the Internet outside of school. At the very least, they could use computers at a public library, but most had access to cell phones, tablets, personal computers, or laptops capable of taking them online. About

Like young people in many countries, Canadian youth frequently connect with friends through social media. Facebook and Twitter are among the most popular sites used by Canada's youth population.

a third of the 5,436 respondents to the survey said they sometimes use the Internet to ask their friends for advice or to seek advice from experts. Teens in the higher grades were most likely to use the Internet to stay in touch with friends through Facebook and Twitter. Ninety-five percent of eleventh-grade students had their own Facebook accounts, and about half maintained Twitter accounts. Teens also said they enjoy posting with their friends on Tumblr, Instagram, and YouTube.

    The connectivity of Canadian teens is not without some drawbacks. One of them is cyberbullying, which occurs even in the most remote parts of Canada. Mary Kathleen Hickox, a senior at Charlottetown Rural High School on Prince Edward Island (PEI), was a victim of Internet bullies when she was younger. That experience led her to join the Royal Canadian Mounted Police National Youth Advisory Committee. She says,

> Here in Charlottetown, P.E.I., the biggest issue facing my fellow youth is cyberbullying. Not only have I been affected by such crimes, most of my friends and peers have as well. In a world where everything evolves and is fluid, our perceptions of bullying must change as well. Bullying is no longer something that can be observed in a school cafeteria; it is invisible. It's on your phone, Facebook, Twitter, computer—it's everywhere and there's often no escape. As a youth from the millennial generation, I can tell you that bullying isn't only common, it's a crisis.[37]

Teens Too Connected

In 2015 the Vancouver-based telecommunications company Telus commissioned a survey on cyberbullying in Canada. Among its findings were that in the month before the survey was taken, 42 percent of the participants said they had been cyberbullied. Moreover, 60 percent of the participants knew someone else who had been victimized.

Another teen who has endured Internet harassment is Mackenzie Murphy, who grew up in Airdrie, Alberta, a small city of about sixty-one thousand people not far from Calgary. Mackenzie's troubles began when she was in fifth grade and continued into her teenage years. Her anonymous critics left brutal messages online for her. She says, "They told me I'm worthless, that no one's ever going to love me. Those feelings of helplessness and not having any idea why you're being attacked—it's hard."[38] Mackenzie has used her experiences with bullying to encourage her city council to pass an antibullying measure that may prevent future outbreaks in her city.

> "Here in Charlottetown, P.E.I., the biggest issue facing my fellow youth is cyberbullying. Not only have I been affected by such crimes, most of my friends and peers have as well."[37]
>
> —Mary Kathleen Hickox, high school senior

Singer Shawn Mendes Is Proud to Call Toronto Home

In many ways, Shawn Mendes is just like any Canadian teenage boy. Raised in suburban Toronto in a town called Pickering along with younger sister Aahyah, Mendes spent a lot of time on social media. One of his favorite apps was Vine, where he posted multiple short videos in which he played guitar while singing famous cover songs. He did so for fun after teaching himself guitar only six months before. The videos caught the attention of a record executive, and Mendes landed a record contract that led to his best-selling album *Handwritten*. He has toured with Taylor Swift and now has 6 million Twitter followers. Mendes tries not to let the trappings of superstardom affect him. He still calls Pickering home:

> It's nice to come back there. With the life I live and always moving, [Pickering] is a little suffocating at times, but it's also the most comforting place in the world. . . . I was an average student. I wasn't any stand out. I remember when people started to know who I was and the label offers [came], people started to get a little weird and be weird around me. But now when I go back, people are fine.

Quoted in Brittany Spanos, "Shawn Mendes: How a Toronto Teen Became the Superstar Next Door," *Rolling Stone*, April 13, 2016. www.rollingstone.com.

Cyberbullying aside, when it comes to the overall use of the Internet, many Canadian teens who participated in the survey concede they may be spending too much time on devices and less time in face-to-face contact with friends. For instance, more than half of the eleventh-grade students were so concerned that they would miss messages from their friends that they sleep with their cell phones. And about 33 percent admitted that they should probably spend less time online than they presently do. But even so, all the students in the survey said they do make time to hang out with friends, participate in family activities, read, and do other fun activities.

Group Dating

Among the activities that appeal to young Canadians is dating. Tweens and teens typically start out by going out on group

Group dates, in which a few friends go on outings together, are often seen as a more comfortable alternative to one-on-one dating. This is especially so for younger teens.

dates, which they regard as a comfortable first step before one-on-one dating starts around age sixteen. Katie, a fifteen-year-old from Carleton Place, Ontario, says, "When you're going out with someone, it's much easier to be yourself when your friends are there, too. If you pretended to be somebody else, your friends would go, 'Whoa, why are you acting so weird?'"[39] For young Canadians, group dates may include trips to the movies, dinner together at casual restaurants, or trips to the local mall.

These early dating relationships tend to follow certain rules about socially acceptable behavior. Jennifer Connolly, a psychology professor at York University in Toronto and an expert on teen relationships, has identified the rules that govern teenage group dating. For example, she points out that girls do not have to wait for boys to ask them out—they can initiate the relationship. However, when it comes to formalizing whether or not the two are a couple, that is typically the boy's decision. Group rules also limit the amount of physical affection a couple can show in front of their friends. Hugging, holding hands, and small kisses are fine, but anything more invites being teased by the group. Finally, she says, there are group prohibitions against dating more than one person at the same time. Brett, a teen from Aurora, Ontario, says that "if a guy's going out with a lot of girls, people will look at him and go, 'You tool, what are you doing?' It lowers your status."[40]

Whether they follow the rules or not, most early teenage dating relationships are short-lived. Some research suggests that they fizzle out after about four months, with so-called long relationships lasting as much as a year. Oftentimes the breakup is amicable, if not mutual, and after a short time both people go on to date others. As Connolly explains, "More often than not, breakups are neutral-positive or learning experiences. Only a minority of cases are upsetting. Usually [the boy or girl] knows why the relationship ended and [they] usually feel they had a role in ending it."[41]

> "When you're going out with someone, it's much easier to be yourself when your friends are there too. If you pretended to be somebody else, your friends would go, 'Whoa, why are you acting so weird?'"[39]
>
> —Katie, a teen from Carleton Place, Ontario

Fewer Canadian Teens Behind the Wheel

As Canadian teens grow older, they eventually leave group dating behind and go out on private dates with their boyfriends and girlfriends. In prior years, going out on dates often required a car and a driver's license. (In most provinces, Canadian teens can get a learner's permit to drive a car shortly before they turn sixteen. In Alberta, learner's permits are available to teens as young as fourteen.) But having a driver's license is not as common among young people as it used to be. In Alberta during the 1990s, for example, 90 percent of residents aged fifteen through twenty-five held driver's licenses. The Alberta government now reports that only about 75 percent of people in that age range have obtained driver's licenses. Experts point to several factors to explain the decline. Alberta driving instructor Ron Wilson attributes millennials' disinterest in driving to the high costs of owning, insuring, maintaining, and fueling automobiles as well as the easy access to public transportation in cities.

Emma O'Neill, twenty-three, still does not have a driver's license, although as a teen she did learn how to drive. She grew up in Arnprior, Ontario, which is about an hour's drive from Ottawa, a big city where exciting entertainment beckoned. But even that lure did not provide incentive enough. She found learning to drive her father's large truck too scary and abandoned the effort. After high school she moved to Toronto, where she did not need a car to get around. "I don't really have any friends who drive cars,"[42] she says. Alya Jinah waited until she was nearly thirty to get her license and did so only because her job in Calgary requires her to drive throughout the city. "I never felt the need for a car," she says. "Basically I lived close to public transit and it was really easy to get around."[43]

Many young people feel strongly about preserving the environment, and they point out that most cars burn gasoline, a fossil fuel that contributes to global warming. They believe that biking, taking public transportation, walking, or sharing rides with others are hallmarks of a more sustainable life. A 2017 study commissioned by the consumer electronics company Canon Canada found that 70 percent of Canadian young people between the ages of fourteen and nineteen do not believe their government is doing enough to protect the environment. "It is very reassuring to see that the majority of Canada's youth are aware of the importance of conserving and improving our environment," said Stan Skorayko, vice president of Canon Canada. "Today's teenagers will be tomorrow's leaders and it is crucial that they continue to view our environment as a high priority in order to ensure that Canada remains an environmental leader in the decades to come."[44]

The fact that young Canadians are interested in issues such as preservation of the environment illustrates that they take life very seriously. Nevertheless, young people in Canada do engage in many leisure activities. Whether they spend their time playing hockey, ringette, or curling or going out on group dates, there are plenty of opportunities for young people in Canada to enjoy life, make friends, and experience all the good times their country has to offer.

CHAPTER FIVE

Hopes and Challenges

Canadian teenagers are optimistic about their lives and futures. A recent survey conducted by Statistics Canada found that teenagers reported experiencing more life satisfaction than Canadians in other age groups. In fact, 94 percent of teens said they were happy. Optimistic teens look forward to futures that offer good jobs, home ownership, marriage, and children.

Even as they work toward their long-term goals, some Canadian teens face serious life challenges. Drug and alcohol addiction, suicide, teen pregnancy, and sexually transmitted diseases afflict Canadian young people in cities and rural areas. Gay, lesbian, and transsexual youth also struggle with some of these issues, in addition to just trying to fit in. And young people of the First Nation communities are still dealing with problems of previous generations, who were forced to live on reservations and attend schools that did not teach them about their heritage or native languages. In many cases First Nation youths endure an unending cycle of poverty.

Liberal Laws Reflect Canadian Views

Canadians, overall, have fairly liberal views on social issues, and this can be seen in some of the country's laws—particularly those that regulate alcohol consumption by young people. In most provinces and territories, for instance, nineteen-year-olds are allowed to buy beer and other alcoholic beverages. In Alberta, Quebec, and Manitoba, the legal drinking age is eighteen. Moreover, in those provinces seventeen-year-olds are permitted to drink as long as they do it at home under their parents' supervision. When it comes to young people and alcoholic beverages, such laws run counter to conventional thinking elsewhere, particularly in the United States, where buying and consuming alcohol under the age of twenty-one has been illegal since 1984.

Lawmakers have adopted such liberal policies under the belief that if Canadians learn to drink responsibly as young people, they will be less likely to abuse alcohol. Indeed, many people continue to advocate for further lowering the drinking age in Canada. In a 2015 column, Kelly Running, the editor of the Saskatchewan newspaper the *Carlyle Observer*, called for the provincial legislature to lower the legal drinking age to eighteen. She said, "Youth still get a hold of alcohol regardless of the drinking age, but perhaps normalizing alcohol consumption by promoting responsibility and moderation will stop binge drinking which is very typical of high school youth and college youth."[45]

Alcohol Abuse

There is no question that many young Canadians do abuse alcohol—consuming beer and other drinks before they reach the legal drinking ages in their provinces and territories. According to a recent study by Project Teen Canada, which has been surveying Canadian teens for more than thirty years, 70 percent of teens admit to illegal drinking. Moreover, a separate study by Teen Challenge, a Canadian group fighting substance abuse, reported that in Saskatchewan, 23 percent of fourteen-year-olds and 70 percent of seventeen-year-olds admitted to drinking five or more drinks within a two-hour period at least once in the past month. "This is a major mental health and public health issue. These really vulnerable children are exposing themselves to very risky behaviours,"[46] says Esme Fuller-Thomson, a University of Toronto professor of social work who has studied binge drinking by young people.

And so young Canadians find themselves living in a society that has written its laws to encourage them to learn to drink responsibly—but many still admit to abusing alcohol. Nevertheless, despite the sta-

> "My parents' opinion has always been a huge thing in my life. It's not so much the punishment I would get if they found out I'd been drinking. It's that, if I ever disappoint them, it makes me feel like, weird."[47]
>
> —Ottawa resident Asia Reid

Young boys from the First Nation Innu community of Natuashish in the Canadian province of Newfoundland and Labrador find ways to entertain themselves on a cold, sunny day.

tistics that would suggest that underage drinking is widespread in Canada, many young people believe they do make the right decisions. For example, when Ottawa resident Asia Reid was fifteen, she talked about going to parties and having no trouble saying no to alcohol. "My parents' opinion has always been a huge thing in my life," she says. "It's not so much the punishment I would get if they found out I'd been drinking. It's that, if I ever disappoint them, it makes me feel like, weird."[47]

Asia says a lot of young people she knows who are focused on doing well in school find ways to resist the temptation to drink; they do not want to risk their futures by becoming dependent on alcohol or face arrest for underage drinking or driving while intoxicated. Asia says young people who drink irresponsibly in Canada are less focused on academics and seeking successful futures for themselves.

Legalizing Marijuana

Canada's laws regarding alcohol can be regarded as liberal, and in the near future the nation's marijuana laws likely will be among the most liberal in the world. In 2017 Canadian prime minister Justin Trudeau proposed legalizing recreational cannabis throughout the country. Bill Blair, a lawmaker and former Toronto police chief, says simply arresting young people and charging them with drug possession has not reduced their desire to use marijuana. "Criminal prohibition has failed to protect our kids and our communities,"[48] says Blair, who supports the legislation.

Under the proposed legislation, users will have to be at least eighteen years old to buy and consume cannabis legally. That means that younger teens who smoke pot would still be using the substance illegally. According to the World Health Organization (WHO), 28 percent of fifteen-year-olds in Canada admit to

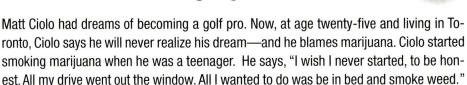

The Downside to Getting High

Matt Ciolo had dreams of becoming a golf pro. Now, at age twenty-five and living in Toronto, Ciolo says he will never realize his dream—and he blames marijuana. Ciolo started smoking marijuana when he was a teenager. He says, "I wish I never started, to be honest. All my drive went out the window. All I wanted to do was be in bed and smoke weed."

Ciolo is one of many Canadians who smoked marijuana during their teen years. Many teens say they use the drug because they like how they feel when they are high. But it is not a harmless pastime. The Canadian Center on Substance Abuse says marijuana can impair a teenager's memory, limit attention spans, stifle the desire to achieve, cause respiratory problems, and impair motor skills.

Some experts are predicting that Canada will soon make recreational marijuana legal, but even then the drug will still be illegal for those under eighteen. As it is, young people are more prone to making impulsive decisions that can lead to unprotected sex, pregnancies, and sexually transmitted diseases; and they are even more likely to do so while under the influence of drugs.

Quoted in Chris Brown and Chris Corday, "Marijuana Research Not Reaching Canada's Toking Teens," *CBC News*, May 18, 2016. www.cbc.ca.

smoking marijuana. Moreover, WHO reports that the present level of marijuana use by Canadian teens is greater than that of any other developed country. "They feel it's not a drug, that it's not harmful. It's not going to hurt me. Part of it is probably because it's smoked and not injected—they don't see it as a chemical since it's not a pill,"[49] says John Westland, a social worker for the substance abuse program at the Hospital for Sick Children in Toronto. Twenty-four-year-old Samantha Martinuk agrees with Westland's assessment. "I smoked weed all through university and I was on the dean's list the entire time," she says. "It didn't turn me into a dead-brained person, like most people say."[50]

Some young people in Canada believe, however, that even if the law does change and pot is legalized, most underage young people who already use the drug will continue to use it. Under the proposed law, people will be able to grow small amounts of marijuana at home or buy the product at licensed and regulated dispensaries. However, some young people predict that marijuana will still be available on the street, and that is where they will keep buying it. "I don't see how legalizing weed will make much of a difference in terms of limiting access to those under the legal age, since it's already so widely available to kids as young as Grade 8 or 9,"[51] says Todd Goncalvez, an eighteen-year-old from Toronto.

Teen Pregnancy and STDs

Just as underage drinking and marijuana use is common among young people in Canada, so is sex. According to a recent study by Statistics Canada, 43 percent of Canadians between the ages of fifteen and nineteen have engaged in sexual relations at least once.

Of course, a major consequence of premarital sex among young people is teenage parenthood. Kristen, who grew up in a poor section of Hamilton, Ontario, had given birth to three children by age twenty. Her journey into motherhood has been difficult. She gave her first baby up for adoption, and an Ontario social services agency has taken the other two children from her. Still, she hopes to go to college one day and win back custody of her two children. Surprisingly, now that she is living on her own and has completed high school, she has no regrets. "I can't complain because it made me out to be who I am today,"[52] she says.

With nearly half of young people in Canada engaging in sex, it should not come as a surprise that the Public Health Agency of Canada has reported an increase in sexually transmitted diseases (STDs) among teens. In 2012, for example, the agency reported that the chlamydia rate among women age nineteen and younger climbed by about 20 percent when compared to 2003 statistics; for men in that age group, the chlamydia rate climbed by about 45 percent.

Catherine Maser, a pediatric nurse at the Hospital for Sick Children, says the level of sex education provided to young people differs from school to school and province to province. These differences may account for why some teens in Canada act re-

A Toronto teen mom travels with her baby every day to school in hopes of completing her education. Many Canadian teens are sexually active and attend sex education classes in schools.

sponsibly but others contract STDs or become pregnant. "It's not standardized and it depends on the teacher and what they are comfortable with teaching," Maser says of sex education in Canada. "It also depends on the school."[53]

In fact, sex education is taught throughout Canada, but there is a wide variation in what is taught and when it is taught. In Ontario, for example, seventh-grade students in public schools learn about STDs. Methods of birth control are taught in public schools in British Columbia in the sixth grade. In Alberta, birth control is discussed in the eighth grade, and students in Saskatchewan learn about it in the ninth grade. The concept of sexual consent is taught as early as the fifth grade in Manitoba.

Some high school students find sex education class valuable, but others do not see the point. Ryan is now twenty-five, but when he was eighteen the Toronto resident said in an interview, "This year, I had a teacher who didn't shy away from anything. I'm so glad, because I don't want to go into a situation clueless."[54] Twenty-five-year-old Kate took the opposite view when she was interviewed at seventeen. The Toronto resident said, "Our teachers brought in a wooden penis, and we took turns putting condoms on it. It was painfully awkward. I learned a lot more from my friends and family."[55] Meanwhile, other schools focus on abstinence. "I went to a Catholic high school," said Eve, who was fifteen at the time. "They basically said abstain. They didn't say if you do have sex, use a condom, nothing like that. It was just 'Don't do it. You shouldn't be doing it. You're too young. It's a sin.' Getting a sexually transmitted disease wasn't even an issue. No one ever brought that up at school with my peers or with the teachers."[56]

LGBTQ Teens

Just as the degree of sex education differs from school to school in Canada, so does the degree to which young Canadians learn about gay rights. Although Canada has been a pioneering country when it comes to gay rights, lesbian, gay, bisexual, transgender, and questioning (LGBTQ) teens often face difficulties fitting in with their peers and lack of support from their parents. The first national climate survey on homophobia in Canadian schools, released in 2011 (the latest year available), found that many LGBTQ teens had been physically or verbally harassed at school and did not feel safe when there. For example, when Marion Miller was fourteen and already beginning to question her own sexuality, she knew one thing for certain: at her school in rural Nova Scotia, kids who had come out were treated poorly. She says, "People would say things like, 'My cousin, I don't talk to him anymore since he came out' and 'There's not any gay people at this school because we would have rounded them up already.'. . . I was shaken. It was really scary. I was like, 'Wow, does this mean I could never come out? Is this what faces me in the world, these kinds of people?'"[57]

Even heterosexual students who took part in the survey were aware of inappropriate comments made to gay students about their sexuality, including comments made by parents and teachers. According to the survey, 70 percent of the more than thirty-seven hundred participants reported hearing such putdowns about their sexuality nearly every day. In addition, LGBTQ students said they felt they were particularly vulnerable to insults and injuries while changing in school locker rooms or visiting school bathrooms.

The level of harassment that students experience varies by school, and some schools do manage to create a healthier environment for all students. Students who attend schools in which there are Gay-Straight Alliance clubs help create more welcoming atmospheres for students of all sexual orientations. Club membership is open to gay, straight, lesbian, and transgender students, and the club is overseen by a faculty adviser. Canadian teens who go to schools in which there is a greater acceptance of LGBTQ students are more likely to be themselves in front of their peers. This may involve dressing in accordance with their sexual identity and being honest about whom they are dating. On the other hand, students who are verbally harassed, physically abused, and belittled by teachers and parents because of their sexuality sometimes suffer shame, loneliness, and depression. Many of these young people often turn to suicide.

Teenage Suicide

According to Statistics Canada, about five hundred people between the ages of ten and twenty-four commit suicide every year. Moreover, many more teenagers think about killing themselves or

Global Citizens

Canadian teens are proud of their country but are eager to see the world as travelers and employees. In a survey by PwC, an international consulting firm, 71 percent of Canadian millennials said they hope to work in another country at some point in their careers. In addition, 68 percent of those surveyed said they would be willing to work in less-developed countries in order to gain experience in commerce.

The pull of this global generation is felt by twenty-three-year-old Jean Gilles, a computer science major at Carleton University in Ottawa, who expects that his future might lead him to work in another country. "There's no right and wrong, just experience," he says. "It may be in Ottawa. It may be on Mars—if they have positions on Mars." Gilles grew up in Ottawa and Quebec and is prepared to leave there for better opportunities.

Christable Sarkar does not count herself among those eager to live and work outside of Canada. Having immigrated to Vancouver from Bangladesh at age fifteen, she believes Canada offers the ingredients for a good life: A place where she can have a good home, a satisfying marriage, and a better life than her parents experienced in their impoverished south Asian homeland. She says, "Happiness has different meanings to different people. But somehow having somebody with you, having a family, having a roof over your head, is what we all basically want. I don't think it has anything to do with culture, race or religion."

Quoted in Joanne Laucius, "Millennials and the 'Canadian Dream': What's the Plan?," *Ottawa Citizen*, July 1, 2016. http://ottawacitizen.com.

Quoted in Ken MacQueen, "Youth Survey: Polite, Honest . . . Bigoted? Immigrant Teens Find That Tolerance Goes Both Ways in Canada," *Maclean's*, April 10, 2009. www.macleans.ca.

---

attempt to do so. A survey released in 2016 by the Canadian organization Kids Help Phone found that 22 percent of the thirteen hundred teens who participated in the study reported thinking about taking their own lives. Attempting suicide is much more common among LGBTQ teens than young people in general. In fact, teens whose families reject their sexual orientation are eight times more likely to harm themselves as heterosexual teens are, according to a recent study reported by Egale, a Canadian human rights organization.

Suicide is an even bigger concern for First Nation teenagers, many of whom grow up in communities in which residents are struggling to find jobs and better lives. David Zimmer, the Aboriginal Affairs minister, describes First Nation communities this way: "They are very, very remote, they're small, there's no economy, there is a sense—especially among younger people—of despair, a lack of opportunity and it leads to depression and anxiety."[58]

Sixteen-year-old Rebecca Hookimaw lives in the tiny First Nation community of Attawapiskat in northern Ontario. With just over two thousand residents, Attawapiskat has seen at least a hundred residents take their own lives in recent years. One of them was Rebecca's thirteen-year-old sister, Sheridan. Rebecca has also tried suicide multiple times and now is living with a new kind of pain—the loss of her sibling. In the past, Rebecca turned to alcohol and drugs to deal with the feelings of hopelessness and despair that come with living in a community in which few residents have jobs, drug-addicted parents are not able to put their children's needs first, and housing and living conditions are poor and uninviting.

> "I hope everything changes in Attawapiskat one day, because I have little brothers and I don't want them growing up the way I grew up."[59]
>
> —Rebecca Hookimaw, a First Nation teen from Attawapiskat, Ontario

But Rebecca no longer thinks suicide is a good option. "If you ever think about taking your life away, don't do it," she says. "Suicide ends your pain, but it will go on to somebody else, and it's just going to keep going. . . . I hope everything changes in Attawapiskat one day, because I have little brothers and I don't want them growing up the way I grew up."[59]

Marriage and Children Remain a Priority

The fact that some young Canadians choose to end their own lives suggests they have deep concerns and misgivings about their own lives and futures. Overall, though, most teens are optimistic about the direction of their lives, and they do think a lot about the future. And when these teens think about their futures, most envision spending it with a spouse and raising children.

A *Huffington Post Canada* survey of more than one thousand Canadians between the ages of eighteen and thirty found that 63

Two teens enjoy a sunny day on Granville Island in Vancouver. Surveys show that, overall, Canada's young people are happy with their lives and optimistic about their futures.

percent said they want to marry at some point in their lives. They are more likely to wait to find that mate until they are older; in Canada, the average age for getting married is 29 for women and 31 for men. Waiting until they are older gives them the chance to finish their postsecondary educations, establish themselves in their careers, and develop the maturity needed to be successful parents.

Jared and Miranda Walker married when they were twenty-four and twenty, respectively. The timing just felt right for them. "As I got to know him [Jared], it became clear to me that if we did get married, our lives would very easily come together, and I wouldn't have to sacrifice anything,"[60] Miranda says. They hope to be parents one day.

As with marriage, most Canadian teens will likely not be parents until at least their late twenties. According to the public opinion research organization Pew Research, the average age for first-time motherhood in Canada is slightly more than twenty-eight years old—an age that is three years older than that of first-time US mothers. Today in Canada more babies are being born to women well into their thirties than to women in their twenties. Young Canadians are increasingly taking their time building their futures before settling down.

Amanda Wilkins has a different vision for her future. She is placing her emphasis on motherhood first. The twenty-six-year-old, who has been married for three years, says, "I always knew I wanted to have kids and be a stay-at-home mom. I understand why women want to go into their careers—my dad was always very business-minded with me—but that for me was always a fallback."[61]

Envisioning the Future

To many Canadian teens, starting their own families is part of the bright futures they envision for themselves. When the Canadian Education Association surveyed one thousand students in the ninth through twelfth grades in 2017, 73 percent agreed that in the next five years they expect new opportunities to come their way. They also expect to earn more money and have greater success than their parents. In all, 84 percent of them said they had set goals for their futures that they expected to achieve. The survey reported that "young people continue to be optimistic about their personal futures. Some think this means that today's youth are better equipped to deal with uncertainty than previous generations. Young people are hopeful and hope has transformative powers."[62]

Teen optimism aside, some experts believe teenagers may have to work harder than their parents did to achieve home ownership, pay for their children's university educations, and fund their own retirements. According to research from the Bank of Montreal

> "Young people continue to be optimistic about their personal futures. Some think this means that today's youth are better equipped to deal with uncertainty than previous generations."[62]
>
> —Canadian Education Association survey

Wealth Institute, an investment services company, teens will have to work more years and save more money than their parents did to make good on their dreams of financial success. Still, more than half of Canadian millennials are already home owners; that is an impressive figure when compared to the home-ownership rates of American millennials—just 36 percent.

Although they face many challenges, young people in Canada hope to lead good and productive lives. Moreover, they want those lives to allow them to contribute to society through work and volunteerism, pass on their values to the children they raise, and continue the work that must be done to eliminate the social problems that lead to poverty, discrimination, addiction, and suicide.

SOURCE NOTES

Chapter One: Where Differences Are Celebrated

1. Quoted in Guy Lawson, "Trudeau's Canada, Again," *New York Times Magazine*, December 8, 2015. www.nytimes.com.
2. Quoted in Stacey Jenkins, "Borders & Heritage: Canada vs. America: My Personal Story," KCTS 9, April 29, 2016. https://kcts9.org.
3. Quoted in Josh Aldrich, "Celebrate Canada's Complete History: Lecture," *Camrose Canadian*, February 16, 2017. www.camrosecanadian.com.
4. Quoted in Chris Frey, "'I'm Moving to Canada': The Cops, Pop Stars, and Athletes Who Made Good on the Threat," *Guardian*, December 14, 2016. www.theguardian.com.
5. Quoted in Sarah Beosveld, "What It's Actually like to Be a Muslim Girl in Canada," *Chatelaine*, February 17, 2017. www.chatelaine.com.
6. Quoted in Beosveld, "What It's Actually like to Be a Muslim Girl in Canada."

Chapter Two: Families in Transition

7. Ontario Human Rights Commission, "The Changing Face of Canadian Families," March 30, 2005. www.ohrc.on.ca.
8. Quoted in Sydney Loney, "The Multi-generational Home Makes a Comeback," *Globe and Mail*, January 20, 2011. www.theglobeandmail.com.
9. Quoted in Doug Neuman, "Free Family Fun with Fire and Ice," *St. Albert Gazette*, February 10, 2016. www.stalbertgazette.com.
10. Quoted in Lia Codrington, "The Path to Team Canada," Hockey Canada, March 15, 2013. www.hockeycanada.ca.
11. Quoted in Dorothy Ratusny, "Getting Deep 15: Pressure to Have Sex, Regaining Trust, Bullies," *Faze*, 2017. http://faze.ca.

12. Quoted in Jason Fekete, "Step-Families Becoming the New Normal in Canada: 2011 Census," *National Post*, September 19, 2012. http://news.nationalpost.com.
13. Quoted in Michelle McQuigge, "Daily Grind of Blended Families a Growing Challenge: Census," *Globe and Mail*, September 19, 2012. www.theglobeandmail.com.
14. Quoted in Sharon Jayson, "Each Family Dinner Adds Up to Benefits for Adolescents," *USA Today*, March 24, 2013. www.usatoday.com.
15. Quoted in Astrid Van Den Broek, "Sharing a Bedroom," *Parents Canada*, October 4, 2010. www.parentscanada.com.
16. Quoted in Michelle Houlden, "Rural vs. Urban Teens: Spot the Difference," *Western Producer*, March 4, 1999. www.producer.com.
17. Quoted in Houlden, "Rural vs. Urban Teens."
18. Quoted in Houlden, "Rural vs. Urban Teens."
19. Quoted in Houlden, "Rural vs. Urban Teens."
20. Quoted in Houlden, "Rural vs. Urban Teens."
21. Quoted in Houlden, "Rural vs. Urban Teens."
22. Quoted in Jonathon Gatehouse, "Youth Survey: City vs. Country Kids," *Maclean's*, April 2, 2009. www.macleans.ca.
23. Quoted in Gatehouse, "Youth Survey."

Chapter Three: Education and Work

24. Quoted in Caroline Alphonso, "Canadian Teens Ace OECD Problem-Solving Test," *Globe and Mail*, April 1, 2014. www.theglobeandmail.com.
25. Quoted in Emma Teitel, "Canada's Future Leaders of 2014," *Maclean's,* April 14, 2014. www.macleans.ca.
26. Jackie Allen, "A Day in the Life: Canada," *Time for Kids*, 2016. www.timeforkids.com.
27. Quoted in Simona Siad, "Canadian Teens Ranked the Hardest Working," *Toronto Star*, May 24, 2007. www.thestar.com.
28. Quoted in Carson Jerema, "Your Grades Will Drop," *Maclean's*, July 8, 2010. www.macleans.ca.
29. Quoted in Evelyn Harford, "The Canadian Dream: Trades a Path to Steady, Reliable Income for Some," *Ottawa Citizen*, July 1, 2016. http://ottawacitizen.com.

30. Quoted in Erin Millar, "The Expectation Gap: Students' and Universities' Roles in Preparing for Life After Grad," *Globe and Mail*, October 11, 2014. www.theglobeandmail.com.
31. Quoted in Dave Dormer, "Youth Hiring Fair Attracts Thousands to Stampede Park," CBC News, March 29, 2017. www.cbc.ca.

Chapter Four: Social Life

32. Quoted in *Leduc Rep,* "Local Ringette Player Amped to Compete at Canadian Ringette Championships," March 15, 2017. www.leducrep.com.
33. Quoted in Andrew Halipchuk, "Ringette Team Earns Silver at Western Championships," *Airdrie City View*, April 6, 2017. www.airdriecityview.com.
34. Quoted in Nick Faris, "Canadian Childhood," *National Post*, 2017. http://news.nationalpost.com.
35. Quoted in Eric Duhatschek, "A Passing of the Broom: Curling Runs in the Family at the Junior Championships," *Globe and Mail*, January 20, 2017. www.theglobeandmail.com.
36. David Berry, "*Degrassi*'s Enduring Popularity Proves Teenagers Will Never Get Tired of Their Honest Reflection," *National Post*, January 14, 2016. http://news.nationalpost.com.
37. Quoted in Royal Canadian Mounted Police, "What's the Biggest Social Issue Facing Youth in Your Community," July 3, 2015. www.rcmp-grc.gc.ca.
38. Quoted in Shawn Logan, "Cyberbulling in Canada: 'It Started When I Was in Grade 5. . . . I'm Proud to Call Myself a Survivor,'" *National Post*, December 18, 2016. http://news.nationalpost.com.
39. Quoted in Marcia Kaye, "Teen Dating," *Today's Parent*, January 18, 2013. www.todaysparent.com.
40. Quoted in Kaye, "Teen Dating."
41. Quoted in Kaye, "Teen Dating."
42. Quoted in Kate Lunau, "For Today's Youth, Cars No Longer Represent Freedom," *Maclean's*, June 5, 2012. www.macleans.ca.
43. Quoted in Rachel Maclean, "Driver's Licenses Not a Priority, Say Some Young Albertans," CBC News, August 5, 2014. www.cbc.ca.

44. Quoted in CNW, "Survey Reveals Seven in 10 Canadian Teens Want More Action Taken on Environment," April 20, 2017. www.newswire.ca.

Chapter Five: Hopes and Challenges

45. Kelly Running, "Drop the Drinking Age," *Carlyle Observer*, June 12, 2015. www.carlyeobserver.com.
46. Quoted in Michael Lyons, "Binge Drinking Among Middle School Children in Canada 'a Major Public Health Issue' and Gay and Lesbian Teens at Highest Risk," *National Post*, May 9, 2014. http://news.nationalpost.com.
47. Quoted in Charlie Gillis, "Youth Survey, Generation Tame," *Maclean's*, April 10, 2009. www.macleans.ca.
48. Quoted in Ian Austen, "Trudeau Unveils Bill Legalizing Recreational Marijuana in Canada," *New York Times*, April 13, 2017. www.nytimes.com.
49. Quoted in Ann Hui, "Canadian Teens Lead Developed World in Cannabis Use: Unicef Report," *Globe and Mail,* April 15, 2013. www.theglobeandmail.com.
50. Quoted in Chris Brown and Chris Corday, "Marijuana Research Not Reaching Canada's Toking Teens," CBC News, May 21, 2016. www.cbc.ca.
51. Quoted in Nicole Thompson, "Teens Say Pot Legalization Won't Change Their Opinions on Weed," *Toronto Star*, April 15, 2017. www.thestar.com.
52. Quoted in *Hamilton Spectator*, "Mothers Too Soon," November 19, 2011. www.thespec.com.
53. Quoted in AboutKidsHealth, "STIs Up, Teen Pregnancy Down in Canada," May 22, 2010. www.aboutkidshealth.ca.
54. Quoted in *Toronto Life*, "Teenage Sex and the City," July 23, 2010. http://torontolife.com.
55. Quoted in *Toronto Life*, "Teenage Sex and the City."
56. Quoted in Anrenée Englande and Gerry Rasmussen, *Dear Diary, I'm Pregnant: Teenagers Talk About Their Pregnancy*. Toronto, ON: Annick, 2010. Kindle edition.
57. Quoted in Melanie Patten, "Small-Town Gay Teens Strive for Big-City Diversity and Acceptance," *Canadian Press,* February 11, 2010.

58. Quoted in Elahe Izadi, "'Need Your Prayers': The Youth-Suicide Crisis Gripping a Canadian Community," *Washington Post*, April 13, 2016. www.washingtonpost.com.
59. Quoted in Colin Perkel, "Attawapiskat Teen Who Lost Sister to Suicide Searches for Meaning," *Hamilton Spectator*, April 24, 2016. www.thespec.com.
60. Quoted in Arti Patel and Rebecca Zamon, "Marriage and Millennials: Why Do Generation Y Couples Say 'I Do' to Matrimony?," *Huffington Post Canada*, February 18, 2013. www.huffingtonpost.ca.
61. Quoted in Patel and Zamon, "Marriage and Millennials."
62. Quoted in *Education Canada*, "Young People's Confidence, Community, and the Future: Why It Matters and What We Can Do About It," Spring 2017. www.cea-ace.ca.

FOR FURTHER RESEARCH

Books
Conrad Black, *Rise to Greatness: The History of Canada from the Vikings to the Present*. Toronto, ON: McClelland & Stewart, 2014.

Charlotte Gray, *The Promise of Canada: 150 Years—People and Ideas That Shaped Our Country*. Toronto, ON: Simon & Schuster Canada, 2016.

Mina Kelly, *Amazing Pictures and Facts About Canada*. Seattle: CreateSpace, 2016.

Christopher Moore, *The Big Book of Canada: Exploring the Provinces and Territories*. Toronto, ON: Tundra, 2017.

Mike Myers, *Canada*. Toronto, ON: Doubleday Canada, 2016.

Alexandra Shimo, *Invisible North: The Search for Answers on a Troubled Reserve*. Toronto, ON: Dundrum, 2016.

Internet Sources
Chris Frey, "'I'm Moving to Canada': The Cops, Pop Stars, and Athletes Who Made Good on the Threat," *Guardian*, December 14, 2016. www.theguardian.com/cities/2016/dec/14/im-moving-to-canada-the-cops-pop-stars-and-athletes-who-made-good-on-the-threat.

Evelyn Harford, "The Canadian Dream: Trades a Path to Steady, Reliable Income for Some," *Ottawa Citizen*, July 1, 2016. http://ottawacitizen.com/news/local-news/the-canadian-dream-trades-a-more-path-to-steady-reliable-income-for-some.

Sydney Loney, "The Multi-generational Home Makes a Comeback," *Globe and Mail*, January 20, 2011. www.theglobeandmail.com/life/relationships/the-multi-generational-home-makes-a-comeback/article570274.

Kate Lunau, "For Today's Youth, Cars No Longer Represent Freedom," *Maclean's*, June 5, 2012. www.macleans.ca/society/technology/for-todays-youth-cars-no-longer-represent-freedom.

Shannon Proudfoot, "Census 2016: A Picture of a Bigger, More Urban Canada," February 8, 2017. www.macleans.ca/news/canada/census-2016-a-picture-of-a-bigger-more-urban-canada.

Websites

Canada 2067 (https://canada2067.ca/en). Canada 2067 is a national initiative promoting science, technology, engineering, and math careers in Canada. Its website has a short animated video that outlines its mission and the prospects for science careers. There is a special section for students interested in science careers and information about youth programs for students in eighth to tenth grade.

Government of Canada (www.canada.ca/en.html). This is the official website for the Canadian government and its agencies. It offers information on how the government works, finding a job, starting a business, travel, immigration, health, citizenship, and more.

Health Canada (www.hc-sc.gc.ca/index-eng.php). Health Canada is the federal agency responsible for keeping Canadians healthy. Its website has information on eating well, immunizations, safety alerts, diseases, and other health topics.

Hockey Canada (www.hockeycanada.ca/en-ca). Hockey Canada is the national governing body for amateur hockey in the country. Its website contains a video on the joys of playing ice hockey, provides links to camps and schools in which ice hockey skills are taught, and offers downloads of core skills.

Statistics Canada (www.statcan.gc.ca). Statistics Canada is the Canadian equivalent of the US Census Bureau. Its website contains census data and reports on topics such as aboriginal peoples, health care, and children and youth.

INDEX

Note: Boldface page numbers indicate illustrations.

Adeniren, Moyo, 42
agriculture, 10
Alberta
   Family Day, 21–22
   legal drinking age, 55–56
   location, **6**
   sex education in, 61
   teens with driving licenses, 53
alcoholic beverages, drinking, 55–57, 64
Allen, Jackie, 33–35
Andrei, Kim, 28
Angus Reid Institute, 17
animal life, 10
apprenticeship programs, 38–39
Asselin, Marie, 29

Bacon, Lindsay, 28–29
Bank of Montreal Wealth Institute, 66–67
Barber, Katherine, 18
Battle of Sainte-Foy, 11
Berry, David, 48
Bibby, Reginald, 30
Blair, Bill, 58
Blandford, Jennifer, 27
blended families, 23–24
Bowman, Brian, 44–45, 46
British Columbia
   Family Day, 21
   location, **6**
   Muslims in, 19
   sex education in, 61
British Commonwealth, 15
Buddhism, increase in number of believers, 17

Canada 2067 (website), 37
Canada, basic facts about, 7
"Canada's Word Lady," 18
Canadian Business (magazine), 40
Canadian Charter of Rights and Freedoms, 14
Canadian Education Association, 66
Canadian football, 46
Canadian Parents for French, 39
Canadian Radio Music Awards, 48
Canadian Ringette Championships, 43
CareerCast, 40
Center for Digital and Media Literacy, 48–49
Cho, Weymi, 16
Ciolo, Matt, 58
cities
   appeal to rural youth of, 28–29
   desire for university education and, 39
   largest, 11
   life in, 27–28, **28**
   See also specific cities
climate, 10–11
colleges and universities, 27, 38
complex stepfamilies, 24
Connolly, Jennifer, 52, 53
crime, 27
culture, shared values, 8
curling, 46–47
currency, **7**, 15
cyberbullying, 49–50

Daigle, Brianne, 36
dating, 51–54, **52**
Dawson, Greg, 26
Deans, Alexander, 31
Degrassi: New Class (television program), 48
divorce, 23
drinking, 55–57
driving, 53–54
drugs, use of, 58–59, 64
Dubois, Catherine, 22–23

Eagle, 63
education
   homeschooling, 34

75

importance of, 31
official languages of, 14
provinces and territories with most adults not having post–high school education, 39
schools, **33**
  attendance policies, 32
  elementary, 32, 33–35
  extracurricular activities, 35
  French immersion, 39
  homophobia in, 61–62
  provincial control of, 32
  quality of, 31, 33
  secondary, 32, 35
  types of, 32–33
  typical day, 32
sex, 60–61
trade, 38–39
Elgar, Frank, 24
Elizabeth II (queen of England), 13, 15
employment
  ability to speak French and, 39
  apprenticeship programs and, 38–39
  desire for, in other countries, 63
  help finding, 41–42
  immediately after high school and university, 40
  jobs in fields certified by CareerCast, 40
  part-time, of teenagers, 36, **36**, 37
England, 11–13, 14
England, Sara, 47
environment, 54

Facebook, popularity of, 49
families
  age for first-time motherhood, 66
  blended, 23–24
  change from traditional structure of, 20
  extended, living together, 20–21
  importance of, 21–22
  marriage, 25, 64–65
  meals together, 24
  in rural areas, 26
  same-sex parents, 25
  siblings sharing rooms, 24–25
Family Day, 21–22, **22**, 23
First Nation people
  conditions in communities, 55, **57**, 64
  conversion of, to Christianity, 16–17
  ice skating by, 44
  name for Canada, 11
  suicide by teenagers, 63–64
flag, **6**
food, 24, 29
Fraser Institute, 34
French and Indian War (1754–1763), 11–12
Fuller-Thomson, Esme, 56

Gale, John, 26–27
Gallup polls, 24
gay rights, 61–62
Gay-Straight Alliance clubs, 62
geography, **6**, **7**, 8–10, **10**
Gilles, Jean, 63
Goncalvez, Todd, 59
government
  administration of territories, 9
  constitution and laws, 14
  described, 7, 13
  role of British monarch, 15
Great Britain, 11–13, 15
group dating, 51–53, **52**

Hickox, Mary Kathleen, 49–50
Hinduism, increase in number of believers, 17
history, 11–13
hockey, 44–46, **45**
home ownership, 67
homophobia, 61–62
Hookimaw, Rebecca, 64
Hookimaw, Sheridan, 64
Horseshoe Falls, 9, **10**
Huffington Post Canada (online newspaper), 64–65

ice skating, 44–45, **45**
iHeartRadio Much Music Video Awards, 27
immigrants, 12, 14–16, **17**
industries, major, 7
Internet
  access to, 48
  cyberbullying on, 49–50
  differences between life in rural areas and cities and, 30
  popularity, **7**
  use, 49, **49**, 51
Ipsos Reid, 37

76

Islam, 17, 18–19

Jacks, Sam, 43
Jinah, Alya, 54
Johnson, Jeff, 31

Kanata, 11
Kaufman, Miriam, 29–30
Kelly, Claire, 44
Kelly, Michaela, 44
Kids Help Phone, 63
Kurdi, Tima, 15–16

Labrador, **6**
languages, 7
    Canadian English, 18
    French immersion schools, 39
    official, 14, 16
Lawson family, 24
lesbian, gay, bisexual, transgender, and questioning (LGBTQ) teens, 61–62
literacy, 7

Manitoba, **6**, 55–56, 61
map, **6**
marijuana, use of, 58–59, 64
marriage, 25, 64–65
Martinuk, Samantha, 59
Maser, Catherine, 60, 61
Mazur, Chris, 38–39
McGill University, 24
McNish, Stuart, 12–13
media and differences between life in rural areas and cities, 30
Mendes, Shawn, 51
Metropolis family, 21
military, 13–14
Miller, Marion, 62
Montreal, 12
Mroz, Bryan, 22
Murphy, Mackenzie, 50
music, 47–48, 51

natural resources, 10
New Brunswick, **6**, 21
Newfoundland, **6**
Niagara Falls, 9, **10**
Northwest Territories, **6**
Nova Scotia, **6**
Nunavut, **6**

O'Neill, Emma, 54
Only in Canada, You Say: A Treasury of Canadian Language (Barber), 18
Ontario
    Education Act, 32
    Family Day, 21
    location, **6**
    percentage bilingual, 16
    population, 11
Ontario Human Rights Commission, 20
Ottawa, **7**, 13

Parker, Clair, 40
Penner, Scott, 38
Pew Research, 66
pond hockey, 21–23
population, 7, 11
premarital sexual relations, 59–61, **60**
Prince Edward Island, **6**
Project Teen Canada, 56
provinces, **6**, 9
    education and, 32, 39
    governments of, 13
    largest, 11
    major cities in, 11
Public Health Agency of Canada, 60
PwC, 63

Quebec
    Battle of Sainte-Foy, 11
    bilingual population in, 16
    French identity of, 12
    legal drinking age, 55–56
    location, **6**
    population, 11
    sugar shacks, 29
Quebec City, **12**

Reid, Asia, 57
religion
    of First Nation people, 16–17
    of immigrants, 17
    Islam, 17, 18–19
ringette, 43–44
Running, Kelly, 56
rural areas
    desire to leave, 28–29
    First Nation communities in, 64
    life in, 25–27, **26**, 29–30
    popularity of trade education, 39
Russon, Randy, 46

Sarkar, Christable, 63
Saskatchewan
  drinking by teenagers in, 56
  Family Day, 21
  location, **6**
  sex education in, 61
Saskatoon, Muslims in, 18
Schafer, Alyson, 24–25
School Sport Canada, 46
sexually transmitted diseases (STDs), 60
sexual relations, 59–61, **60**
Shaw Rocket Fund, 48
shinny, 21–23
Sigvaldason, Nadine, 27
Sikhism, increase in number of believers, 17
Sims, Daniel, 14
Skorayko, Stan, 54
social media, 49–51
Spinks, Nora, 23
sports
  curling, 46–47
  hockey, 44–46, **45**
  ice skating, 44–45
  ringette, 43–44
  shinny, 21–23
Statistics Canada
  number of students attending public schools, 33
  percentage of bilingual population, 16
  percentage of families
    blended, 23
    including extended family member, 20
    same-sex parents, 25
    single parent, 23
    two-parent, 20
  percentage of population living in cities or suburbs, 25
  percentage of teenagers
    engaging in sexual relations, 59
    feeling stressed, 36
    happy, 55
stepfamilies, 23
Suchan, Alyssa, 43
sugar shacks, 29
suicide, 62–64
symbols, 8

Syria, refugees from, 15, **17**

teenagers
  activities of urban, 11
  after high school plans, 37
  age of majority, 13
  cyberbullying and, 49–50
  Internet and social media use by, 49, **49**, 51
  military and, 13–14
  optimism about future, 66
  as parents, 59–61, **60**
  population, 7
  stresses on, 36–38
Teen Challenge, 56
television, 48
Telus, 50
territories, **6**, 9, 39
Toronto, 27
tourism, 9, **10**
towns. See rural areas
trade education, 38–39
Trudeau, Justin, 8, 58
Twitter, popularity of, 49

United States, **6,** 9, 47,
universities, 27, 38

values, 8
Vancouver, 16, **65**
Van Pelt, Deani, 34
voting, 13

Wajahat, Maryann, 18
Walker, Jared, 65
Walker, Miranda, 65
Westland, John, 59
Wilkins, Amanda, 66
Wilson, Ron, 53
Women's World Championship (hockey), 23
World Health Organization (WHO), 58–59
Worts family, 21

young adults. See teenagers
YouTube FanFest, 27
Yukon Territory, **6**

Zimmer, David, 64

PICTURE CREDITS

Cover: iStockphoto/Ivantar

6: Maury Aaseng (map)

6: Shutterstock (flag)

7: Shutterstock.com/Zoryanka (first picture)

7: Shutterstock/Lopolo (second picture)

7: Shutterstock.com/Carpathian Prince (third picture)

7: Shutterstock/Patramansky Oleg (fourth picture)

10: Shutterstock.com/Helen Filatova

12: Shutterstock/Songquan Deng

17: Carlos Osorio/Zuma Press/Newscom

22: Bernard Weil/Zuma Press/Newscom

26: Kymberlie Dozois Photography Image Source/Newscom

28: Shutterstock/GTS Productions

33: Richard Lautens/Zuma Press/Newscom

36: Shutterstock.com/Icatnews

41: Dave Bartruff/Danita Delimont Photography/Newscom

45: iStockphoto/Sierrarat

49: Shutterstock/SpeedKingz

52: Shutterstock/Iakov Filimonov

57: Peter Power/Zuma Press/Newscom

60: Michael Stuparyk/Zuma Press/Newscom

65: Associated Press

ABOUT THE AUTHOR

Gail Snyder is a freelance writer and advertising copywriter who has written more than twenty-five books for young readers. She grew up in Pennsylvania, where she resides with her husband, Hal Marcovitz.